Biotechnology in the 21ˢᵗ Century

The Ethics of Biotechnology

Biotechnology in the 21st Century

Biotechnology on the Farm and in the Factory
Agricultural and Industrial Applications

Biotechnology and Your Health
Pharmaceutical Applications

Bioinformatics, Genomics, and Proteomics
Getting the Big Picture

The Ethics of Biotechnology

Biotechnology in the 21st Century

The Ethics of Biotechnology

Jonathan Morris, Ph.D.

CHELSEA HOUSE
P U B L I S H E R S

CHELSEA HOUSE PUBLISHERS
VP, New Product Development Sally Cheney
Director of Production Kim Shinners
Creative Manager Takeshi Takahashi
Manufacturing Manager Diann Grasse

Staff for THE ETHICS OF BIOTECHNOLOGY
Associate Editor Beth Reger
Editorial Assistant Kuorkor Dzani
Production Editor Bonnie Cohen
Photo Editor Sarah Bloom
Series & Cover Designer Keith Trego
Layout 21st Century Publishing and Communications, Inc.

www.chelseahouse.com

First Printing

9 8 7 6 5 4 3 2 1

Library of Congress Cataloging-in-Publication Data

Morris, Jonathan, PhD.
  The ethics of biotechnology/Jonathan Morris.
    p. cm.—(Biotechnology in the 21st century)
  Includes bibliographical references and index.
  ISBN 0-7910-8520-1
  1. Biotechnology—Moral and ethical aspects—Popular works. I. Title. II. Series.
TP248.23.M67 2005
174'.96606—dc22

                                        2005015384

All links and web addresses were checked and verified to be correct at the time of publication.
Because of the dynamic nature of the web, some addresses and links may have changed since
publication and may no longer be valid.

Table of Contents

Detailed Table of Contents

Foreword

The processes that eventually led to life began inside the first generation of stars that resulted after what astrophysicists refer to as the Big Bang. The events associated with the Big Bang mark the beginning of our universe—a time during which such simple elements as hydrogen and helium were turned by gravitational pressure and heat into carbon, oxygen, nitrogen, magnesium, chlorine, calcium, sodium, sulfur, phosphorous, iron, and other elements that would make the formation of the second generation of stars and their planets possible. The most familiar of these planets, our own planet Earth, would give rise to life as we know it—from cells and giant squids to our own human race.

At every step in the processes that led to the rich variety of life on Earth, the thing that was forming in any particular environment was capable of transforming, and did, transform that environment. Especially effective at transformation was that class of things that we now refer to as replicators. We know of two examples of replicators: genes and memes. (The latter rhymes with "creams.")

Genes and memes exist in cells, tissues, and organs. But memes mostly are in brains, and human religions and civilizations. Near the bottom of the hierarchy it's all genes and near the top it's more memes. Genes appeared independently of cells, and are responsible for most of what we call biological life, which can be thought of as a soft and comfortable vehicle made mostly of cells, and created and maintained by the genes, for their efficient replication and evolution. Amazingly, the existence of replicators is all it takes to explain life on Earth; no grand creation, no intelligent design, no constant maintenance; at first just genetic replicators and natural selection, and as far as we know, just one more thing, which appeared after there were human brains big enough to support them: memes.

Genes you've already heard of; but memes may be a completely new term to you. Memes follow the same rules as genes and their natural selection and evolution account for everything that the natural selection of genes doesn't. For instance, our brains are almost too large for our upright stance and therefore must somehow answer to a calling other than the mere replication of our genes, which were doing okay without the extra pint of white matter we gained in the last 50,000 years. The striking increase in brain size means something powerful is strongly benefiting from our increased brain capacity. The best explanation for this, according to Richard Dawkins, in his best-selling and robustly influential book, *The Selfish Gene*, is that our brains are particularly well adapted for imitation, and therefore for the replication of memes. Memes are things like words, ideas, songs, religious or political viewpoints, and nursery rhymes. Like genes, they exist for themselves—that is, they are not here to promote us or anything else, and their continued existence does not necessarily depend on their usefulness to anything: only to their fecundity, their ability to copy themselves in a very precise, but inexact way, and their relative stability over time. It is these features of **genes** and of **memes** that allow them to take part in natural selection, as described by Darwin in 1859, in spite of the fact that he was unaware of the nature of the two replicators. After 150 years, we have started to understand the details. Looking back on it from only a century and a half, Darwin's conception was probably the most brilliant that mankind has chanced upon in our relatively short time here on Earth. What else could possibly explain dandelions?

Dawkins realized that the genes were evolving here, not us. We are just the vessel, and Dawkins realized the significance of replicators in general. After that, the field opened up rather widely, and must include Stan Cohen and Herbert Boyer, whose notion, compounded in 1973 in a late-night deli in Oahu, of artificially replicating specific genes underlies most of the subject matter in this rather important series of books.

SO WHAT'S SO IMPORTANT ABOUT GENES AND MEMES?

I'm sure that most of you might want to know a little bit about the stuff from which you are made. Reading the books in this series will teach you about the exciting field of biotechnology and, perhaps, most importantly, will help you understand what you are (now pay attention, the following clause sounds trivial but it isn't), *and* give you something very catchy to talk about with others, who will likely pass along the information to others, and so on. What you say to them may outlive you. Reading the books in this series will expose you to some highly contagious memes (recall that memes are words, ideas, etc.) about genes. And you will likely spread these memes, sometimes without even being aware that you are doing so.

THE BIRTH OF BIOTECHNOLOGY—OAHU 1973

So what happened in Oahu in 1973? Taking the long view, nothing really happened. But we rarely take the long view, so let's take the view from the 70s.

At the time, it was widely held that genes belonged to a particular organism from whose progenitors the gene had been passed to an organism and that the organism in question would pass the gene to its offspring, and that's the only way that genes got around. It made sense. Genes were known by then to carry the instructions for building new organisms out of the germinal parts of old organisms, including constructing a wide array of devices for collecting the necessary raw materials needed for the process from the environment; genes were the hereditary mechanism whereby like begat like, and you looked like your parents because of similar genes, rather than looking like your neighbors. The "horizontal transfer" of genes from one species to another was not widely contemplated as being possible or desirable, in spite of the fact that such transfer was already evident in the animal and plant worlds—think of mules and nectarines. And "undesirable" is putting it rather mildly. A lot of people thought it was a horrible idea. I was a research scientist in the recombinant laboratories of Cetus Corporation in 1980, during which time Cetus management prudently did not advertise the location of the lab for fear that the good people of Berkeley, California (a town known for its extreme tolerance of most things) might take offense and torch our little converted warehouse of a lab. Why this problem in regard to hybrid life forms? Maybe it had something to do with the fact that mules were sterile and nectarines were fruit.

Apples have been cultivated in China for at least 4,000 years. The genetic divergence from the parental strains has all been accomplished by intentional cultivation, including selection of certain individuals for properties that appealed to our farming ancestors; and farmers did so without much fanfare. The Chinese farmers were not aware that genes were being altered permanently and that was the reason that the scions from favored apple trees, when grafted onto a good set of roots, bred true. But they understood the result. Better apple genes have thus been continually selected by this process, although the process through-out most of history was not monitored at the genetic level. The farmers didn't have any scary words to describe what they were doing, and so nobody complained. Mules and nectarines and Granny Smith apples were tolerated without anyone giving a hoot.

Not so when some educated biologists took a stab at the same thing and felt the need to talk about it in unfamiliar terms to each other, but not the least to the press and the businessmen who were thinking about buying in. There was, perhaps, a bit too much hyperbole in the air. Whatever it was, nobody was afraid of apples, but when scientists announced that they could move a human gene into a bacterium, and the bacterium would go on living and copying the gene, all hell broke loose in the world of biology and the sleepy little discipline of bioethics became a respectable profession. Out of the settling dust came the biotechnology industry, with recombinant insulin, human growth hormone, erythropoietin, and tissue plas-minogen activator, to name a few.

CETUS IN 1980

The genie was out of the bottle. Genes from humans had been put into terrified bacteria and the latter had survived. No remarkable new bacteremias—that is, diseases characterized by unwanted bacteria growing in your blood—had emerged, and the initial hesitancy to do recombinant DNA work calmed down. Cetus built a P-3, which was something like an indoor submarine, with labs inside of it. The P-3 was a royal pain to get in and out of; but it had windows through which potential investors could breeze by and be impressed by the bio-suited scientists and so, just for the investment it encouraged, it was worth it. Famous people like Paul Berg at Stanford had warned the biotech community that we were playing with fire. It stimulated investment. When nobody died bleeding from the eyeballs, we started thinking maybe it wasn't all that scary. But there was something in the air. Even the janitors pushing their brooms through the labs at night and occasional scientists working until dawn, felt that something new and promising was stirring.

My lab made oligonucleotides, which are little, short, single-stranded pieces of DNA, constructed from the monomers A, C, T, and G that we bought in kilogram quantities from the Japanese, who made them from harvested salmon sperm (don't ask me how). We broke these DNA pieces down into little nucleoside constituents, which we chemically rebuilt into 15- to 30-base long sequences that the biologists at Cetus could use to find the big pieces, the genes, that coded for things like interferons, interleukins, and human proteins.

We were also talking about turning sawdust into petroleum products. The price of petroleum in the world was over \$35 a barrel, if my memory serves me at all, which was high for the decade. A prominent oil company became intrigued with the sawdust to petroleum idea and gave us somewhere between \$30 or \$40 million to get us started on our long-shot idea.

The oil company funding enabled us to buy some very expensive, sensitive instruments, like a mass spectrometer mounted on the backside of a gas chromatograph, now called GCMS. It was possible under very special conditions, using GCMS, to prove that it could be done—glucose could be converted biologically into long chain hydrocarbons. And that's what gasoline was, and sawdust was mainly cellulose, which was a polymer of glucose, so there you have it. Wood chips into gasoline by next year. There were a few details that have never been worked out, and now it has been a quarter of a very interesting century in which the incentive, the price of oil, is still very painful.

My older brother Brent had gone to Georgia Tech as had I. He finished in chemical engineering and I in chemistry. Brent worked for a chemical company that took nitrogen out of the air and methane out of a pipe and converted them into just about anything from fertilizer to the monomers needed to make things like nylon and polyethylene. Brent and I both knew about chemical plants, with their miles of pipes and reactors and about a century of good technical improvements, and that the quantities of petroleum products necessary to slake the global appetite for dark, greasy things would not fit easily into indoor submarines. We had our doubts about the cellulose to oil program, but proteins were a different thing altogether. Convincing bacteria, then later yeasts and insect cells in culture, to make human proteins by inserting the proper genes not only seemed reasonable to us but it was reasonable.

WE DID IT!

I remember the Saturday morning when David Mark first found an *E. coli* clone that was expressing the DNA for human beta-interferon using a P32 labeled 15-base long oligonucleotide probe that my lab had made. Sometimes science is really fun. I also remember the Friday night driving up to my cabin in Mendocino County when I suddenly realized you could make an unlimited amount of any DNA sequence you had, even if what you had was just a tiny part of a complex mixture of many DNAs, by using two oligos and a polymerase. I called it Polymerase Chain Reaction. The name stuck, but was shortened to PCR.

We were down in a really bad part of town, Emeryville being the industrial side of Berkeley; but we were young and brave, and sometimes it was like an extended camping trip. There were train tracks behind our converted warehouse. You could walk down them during the daytime to an Indian restaurant for lunch, or if you could manage to not be run over by a train late at night while a gel was running or an X-ray plate was exposing, you could creep over across the tracks to the adjacent steel mill and watch white hot steel pouring out of great caldrons. In the evenings, you could go up on the roof and have a beer with the president of the company.

Like the Berkeley of the late Sixties which had preceded it, it was a time that would never happen again.

Today, nobody would be particularly concerned about the repercussions of transferring a gene out of bacteria, say a gene out of *Bacillus thuringiensis* inserted into a commercial strain of corn, for instance. Genes now have found a new way to be moved around, and although the concept is not revolutionary, the rate at which it is happening is much faster than our own genes can react to. The driver, which is the case for all social behaviors in humans today, is the meme. Memes can appear, replicate, and direct our actions as fast as thought. It isn't surprising, but it does come as a shock to many people when they are confronted with the undisputed fact that the evolving elements in what we have referred to as biological evolution, which moves us from *Homo habilus* to *Homo sapiens*, are genes; not organisms, packs, species, or kinship groups. The things that evolve are genes, selfishly. What comes as an even more shocking surprise, and which in fact is even less a part of the awareness of most of us, is that our behavior is directed by a new replicator in the world, the meme.

YOU MAY WANT TO SKIP THIS PART
(Unless You're Up for Some Challenging Reading)

Let's digress a little, because this is a lot of new stuff for some people and may take a few hours to soak in. For starters, what exactly is a gene? . . . atgaagtgtgccgtgaaagctgctacgctcgacgctc-gatcacctggaaaaccctggtag . . . could be the symbol for a gene, a rather short gene for our editorial convenience here (most of them have thousands of letters). This rather short gene would code for the peptide met-lys-cys-ala-val-lys-gly-gly-thr-leu-asp-ala-arg-ser-pro-gly-lys-pro-trp, meaning that in a cell, it would direct the synthesis of that string of amino acids, (which may or may not do something very important).

Getting back to the gene, it may share the organism as an environment favoring its replication with a whole gang of other replicators (genes), and they may cooperate in providing a comfy little protected enclave in which all of the genes develop a means to replicate and cast their sequences into the future all using the same mechanism. That last fact is important as it separates a cellular gene from a viral gene, but I won't belabor it here. Reviewing just a little of what I've infected you with, that sequence of AGCT-type letters above would be a replicator, a gene, if it did the following:

(1) exhibited a certain level of fecundity—in other words, it could replicate itself faster than something almost like it that couldn't keep up;

(2) its replication was almost error-free, meaning that one generation of it would be the same as the next generation with perhaps a minor random change that would be passed on to what now would be a branch of its gene family, just often enough to provide some variation on which natural selection could act; and

(3) it would have to be stable enough relative to the generation time of the organism in which it found itself, to leave, usually unchanged, with its companion genes when the organism reproduced.

If the gene goes through the sieve of natural selection successfully, it has to have some specific identity that will be preserved long enough so that any advantage it confers to the rate of its own replication will, at least for some number of generations, be associated with its special identity. In the case of an organic replicator, this specialness will normally be conferred by the linear sequence of letters, which describe according to the genetic code, a linear sequence of amino acids in a peptide. The process is self-catalytic and almost irreversible, so once a sequence exhibits some advantage in either (1), (2), or (3), all other things being nearly equal, it is selected. Its less fortunate brethren are relatively unselected and the new kid on the block takes over the whole neighborhood. See how that works?

This should not be shocking to you, because it is a tautology, meaning it implies nothing new. Some people, however, are accustomed to the notion that genes and individual organisms serve the greater good of something they call a species, because in the species resides an inviolate, private gene pool, which is forever a part of that species. This concept, whether you like it or not, is about as meaningful—and now I guess I will date myself—as the notion that Roger Waters is forever and always going to be playing with Pink Floyd. It isn't so. Waters can play by himself or more likely with another group. So can genes. And don't forget that not only genes, but also an entirely different kind of replicator is currently using our bodies as a base of operations. Genes have a reaction time that is slow relative to the lifetime of an individual. It takes a long time for genes to respond to a new environment. Memes can undergo variation and selection at the speed of thought.

Let's leave the subject of memes for awhile. They are an immense part of every human now, but biotechnology as practiced in the world and described in this book does not pay them much mind. Biotechnologists are of the impression that their world is of genes, and that's alright. A whole lot happened on Earth before anybody even expected that the place was spinning and moving through space, so memes can wait. I thought I ought to warn you.

It is worth noting that new gene *sequences* arise from pre-existing gene sequences but gene *molecules* are not made out of old genes. Gene molecules are made out of small parts that may have been in genes before, but the atoms making up the nucleotides that are strung together and constitute today's incarnation of a gene, may have two weeks ago been floating around in a swamp as urea or flying out of a volcano as hot lava. A gene *sequence* (notice that molecule is not equal to sequence) that makes itself very useful may last millions of years with hardly a single change. You may find precisely the same gene sequence in a lot of very different species with few significant changes because that sequence codes for some protein like cytochrome C that holds an iron atom in a particularly useful way, and everybody finds that they need it. It's a more classic design than a Jaguar XK and it just keeps on being useful through all kinds of climatic eras and in lots of different species. The sequence is almost eternal. On the very different other hand, the specific molecular incarnations of a gene sequence, like the DNA molecule that encodes the cytochrome C sequence in an individual cell of the yeast strain that is used, for example, to make my favorite bread, Oroweat Health Nut, is ephemeral. The actual molecules strung together so accurately by the DNA polymerase to make the cytochrome C are quickly unstrung in my small intestine as soon as I have my morning toast. I just need the carbon, nitrogen, and phosphorous. I don't eat it for the sequence. All DNA sequences taste the same, a little salty if you separate them from the bread.

That's what happens to most chemical DNA molecules. Somebody eats them and they are broken down into general purpose biological building blocks, and find their way into a new and different molecule. Or, as is often the case in a big organism like Arnold Schwarzenegger, body cells kill themselves while Governor Schwarzenegger is still intact because of constantly undergoing perfectly normal tissue restructuring. Old apartments come down, new condos go up, and beautiful, long, perfectly replicated DNA sequences are taken apart brick by brick. It's dangerous stuff to leave around on a construction site. New ones can be made. The energy just keeps coming: the sun, the hamburgers, the energy bars.

But the master sequences of replicators are not destroyed. Few germ cells in a woman's ova and an embarrassingly large number of germ cells in a male's sperm are very carefully left more or less unaltered, and I say more or less, because one of the most important processes affecting our genes, called recombination, does alter the sequences in important ways; but I'm not going to talk about it here, because it's pretty complicated and this is getting to be too long. Now we are ready to go back to the big question. It's a simple answer, but I don't think you are going to get it this year.

If . . . atgaagtgtgccgtgaaagctgctacgctcgacgctcgatcacctggaaaaccct-ggtag . . . is a gene, then what particular format of it is a gene? For this purpose, let's call it a replicator instead of a gene, because all genes are after all replicators. They happen to encode protein sequences under certain conditions, which is one of our main uses for them. As I've mentioned, the one above would code for the protein met-lys-cys-ala-val-lys-gly-gly-thr-leu-asp-ala-arg-ser-pro-gly-lys-pro-trp with the final "tag" being a punctuation mark for the synthesis mechanism to stop. We make other uses of them. There are DNA aptamers, which are single-stranded DNA polymers useful for their three-dimensional structures and ability to specifically cling to particular molecular structures, and then there is CSI, where DNA is used purely for its ability to distinguish between individuals. But *replication* for the genes is their reason for being here. By "reason for being here," I don't mean to imply that they are here because they had some role to fulfill in some overall scheme; I just mean simply that they are here because they replicate—it's as simple or impossible to understand as that. Their normal way of replication is by being in their molecular form as a double stranded helical organic polymer of adenosine, guanosine, thymidine, and cytosine connected with phosphate linkages in a cell. Or they could be in a PCR tube with the right mixture of nucleoside triphosphates, simple inorganic salts, DNA polymerase, and short strands of single-stranded DNA called primers (we're getting technical here, that's why you have to read these books). Looking ahead, DNA polymerase is a molecular machine that hooks the triphosphate form of four molecular pop beads called A, C, T, and G together into long meaningful strings.

Okay, getting back to the question, is the gene, . . . atgaagtgtgccgtgaaagctgctacgctcgacgctcgatcacctggaaaaccctggtag . . . always the organic polymer form of the sequence, which has a definite mass, molecular weight, chemical structure, or is the Arabic letter form of it in your book still a gene, or is the hexadecimal representation of it, or the binary representation of it in your CPU a gene, or is an equivalent series of magnetic domains aligned in a certain way on your hard disk just another form of a gene? It may sound like a dumb question, but it isn't. If you are insistent that a gene is just the organic polymer of A, C, T, and G that can be operated on by DNA polymerase to make replicas in a cell, then you may take a minute to think about the fact that those little triphosphate derivatives of A, C, T, and G may not have been little nucleotides last month when they were instead disembodied nucleotide pieces or even simple atoms. The atoms may have been residing in things called sugars or amino acids in some hapless organism that happened to become food for a bigger organism that contained the machinery that assembled the atoms into nucleotides, and strung them into the sequence of the gene we are talking about. The thing that is the same from generation to generation is the sequence, not the molecule. Does that speak to you? Does it say something like maybe the symbol of the gene is more the gene than the polymer that right now contains it, and the comprehensive symbolic representation of it in any form at all is a replicator? This starts to sound pretty academic, but in any biotechnology lab (and you will read about some of them in this series) making human proteins to sell for drugs, the genes for the proteins take all the above mentioned forms at one time or another depending on what is appropriate, and each of them can be reasonably called a replicator, the gene. Genetic engineering is not just the manipulation of chemicals.

SKIP DOWN TO HERE

These books are not written to be the behind the scenes story of genes and memes any more than a description of an integrated circuit for someone who wants to use it in a device for detecting skin conductivity or radio waves is about quantum mechanics. Quantum mechanics is how we understand what's happening inside of a transistor embedded in an integrated circuit in your iPod or described in the Intel catalogue. By mentioning what's going on inside biotechnology, I hope to spark some interest in you about what's happening on the outside, where biotechnology is, so you can get on about the important business of spreading these memes to your friends. There's nothing really thrilling about growing bacteria that make human hormones, unless your cousin needs a daily injection of recombinant insulin to stay alive, but the whole process that you become involved in when you start manipulating living things for money or life is like nothing I've found on the planet for giving you the willies. And remember what I said earlier: you need something to talk about if you are to fulfill your role as a meme machine, and things that give you the willies make great and easily infectious memes. Lowering myself to the vernacular for the sake of the occasional student who has made it this far, "biotech is far out man." If you find something more interesting, let me know. I'm at kary@karymullis.com, usually.

Dr. Kary B. Mullis
Nobel Prize Winner in Chemistry, 1993
President/Altermune, LLC

Introduction

Biotechnology, the use of biological organisms and processes to provide useful products in industry and medicine, is as old as cheese making and as modern as creating a plant-based energy cell or the newest treatment for diabetes. Every day, newspaper articles proclaim a new application for biotechnology. Often, the media raises alarms about the potential for new kinds of biotechnology to harm the environment or challenge our ethical values. As a result of conflicting information, sorting through the headlines can be a daunting task. These books are designed to allow you to do just that—by providing the right tools to help you to make better educated judgments.

The new biotechnologies share with the old a focus on helping people lead better, safer, and healthier lives. Older biotechnologies, such as making wine, brewing beer, and even making bread, were based on generations of people perfecting accidental discoveries.

The new biotechnologies are built on the explosion of discoveries made over the last 75 years about how living things work. In particular, how cells use genetic material to direct the production of proteins that compose them, and provide the engines used to produce energy needed to keep them alive. These discoveries have allowed scientists to become genetic engineers, enabling them to move genes from one living organism to another and change the proteins made by the new organism, whether it is a bacterium, plant, mouse, or even a human.

Biotechnologists first engineered bacterial cells, producing new proteins useful in medicine and industry. The type of cell that biotechnologists engineer today may be a simple bacterium or a complicated animal or human cell. The protein product might be a simple string of amino acids or a complicated antibody of four chains, with critical genetic instructions from both mice and humans. Plant biotechnologists engineer plants to resist predatory insects or harmful chemicals to help farmers produce more, with less risk and expense. Plants have also been engineered to make products useful for industry and manufacturing. Animals have been engineered for both research and practical uses.

Research is also underway to develop methods of treating human diseases by changing the genetic information in the cells and tissues in a patient's body. Some of these efforts have been more successful than others and some raise profound ethical concerns. Changing the genetic information of a human may one day prevent the development of disease, but the effort to do so pushes the envelope of both ethics and technology. These and other issues raised by advances in biotechnology demand that we as citizens understand this technology, its promise, and its challenge so that we can provide appropriate limits on what biotechnologists create.

Who are the biotechnologists, the genetic engineers? Generally, they have university or advanced training in biology or chemistry. They may work in a university, a research institute, a company, or the government. Some are laboratory scientists trained in the tools of genetic engineering–the laboratory methods that allow a gene for a particular protein to be isolated from one living creature's DNA and inserted into another's DNA in a way that instructs the new cell to manufacture the protein. Some are computer scientists who assemble databases of the DNA and protein sequences of whole organisms. They may write the computer code that allows other scientists to explore the databases and use the information to gain understanding of evolutionary relationships or make new discoveries. Others work in companies that engineer biological factories to produce medicines or industrial plastics. They may engineer plants to promote faster growth and offer better nutrition. A few have legal training that allows them to draft or review patents that are critical to the business of biotechnology. Some even work in forensic laboratories, processing the DNA fingerprinting you see on TV.

The exact number of working biotechnologists is hard to determine, since the job description doesn't neatly fit into a conventional slot. The U.S. Department of Labor indicates that there are over 75,000 Master's and Ph.D.-level biologists in the U.S., and Bio.org, the Website for the Biotechnology Industry Organization, reports nearly 200,000 biotechnologists are currently employed.

Biotechnology is not just the stuff of the future. The work of modern biotechnology and genetic engineering is in our daily lives, from the food we eat and clothing we wear to some of the medicines we take. The ketchup you put on your fries at lunch today may have been sweetened with corn syrup made from corn that was engineered to resist a deadly insect. The cotton in your T-shirt, even if the shirt were made in China or Bangladesh, probably came from a U.S. cotton plant genetically engineered to resist another insect. If someone in your family is a diabetic, the insulin he or she injects and the glucose test monitor used to determine the amount of insulin to inject rely on biotechnology. If you go to the doctor and she arranges for blood tests, the laboratory uses biotechnology products to run those tests.

This series, BIOTECHNOLOGY IN THE 21ST CENTURY, was developed to allow you to understand the tools and methods of biotechnology, and to appreciate the current impact and future applications of biotechnology in agriculture, industry, and your health. This series also provides an exploration of how computers are used to manage the enormous amount of information produced by genetic researchers. The ethical and moral questions raised by the technology, whether they involve changing the genetic information of living things or using cells from human embryos to develop new ways to treat disease, are posed with a foundation in how moral philosophers think about ethical issues. With these tools, you will be better able to understand the headlines about the latest advances in biotechnology and the alarms raised by those concerned with the impact that these applications have on the environment and our society. You may even be inspired to learn more and join the community of scientists who work on finding new and better ways to produce food, products, and medical treatments.

Bernice Zeldin Schacter, Ph.D.
Consulting Editor

1

What World Will We Live In?

Imagine a world where **biotechnology** has been allowed to flourish and fulfill its greatest potential. Biotechnology is using the knowledge we gain by studying living organisms to create useful new products, organisms, and medical treatments. In this imaginary world, the ethical concerns related to biotechnology have been well thought out, and the laws regulating biotechnology are considered fair and moral. Laws and regulations based on this ethical understanding are widely accepted and followed. In this world, the technology exists to regenerate a person's own organs in order to replace ones that have worn out or that are diseased. Degenerative brain diseases like **Alzheimer's** and **Parkinson's disease** can be cured with an injection of engineered cells that replace missing and damaged neurons. People of the world are virtually free of infectious disease, thanks to the creation of effective **vaccines** and **antimicrobial** drugs. A handheld instrument has been developed that reads genetic code from a drop of blood or a strand of hair, and within minutes, points out potential health risks and ways to minimize the chances of developing life-threatening illnesses. When you go to the doctor, personalized medications are prescribed based on your distinct genetic makeup, and these medications are much more effective at curing illnesses than ever before. In this scenario, scientists have **genetically engineered** plants to produce inexpensive medications, while other plants have been engineered to be more nutritious or to grow in inhospitable climates or nutrient-poor soils. Fewer people in the world go hungry. When you are devastated by the death of your favorite pet, you can get a clone that looks exactly like the original, though its personality may be very different because personality is the result of the interactions of an organism's genes within the unique environment in which the organism develops. An oil-based economy has been replaced by one reliant on cleaner, renewable, sources of energy, many of which are biologically based. Today we already use microbes to produce ethanol that can be used to decrease our dependence on gasoline, and to produce methane from garbage that can be collected as another fuel (Figure 1.1).

Now imagine another world where little biotechnology has been developed, one where restrictive laws and overly concerned citizens have prevented biotechnology from fulfilling its potential. A very restrictive standard of ethics has been adopted by society. **Genetic engineering** of plants and animals has been severely restricted or banned. No techniques have been developed to find genetic-based cures for disease. Funding for stem cell research, where special cells of the body can be used to replace diseased tissues, is banned by the federal government, as is funding for any form of cloning. Crops grown by conventional means are unable to keep up with food demands worldwide. Insects have become resistant to most common **pesticides** and are causing large crop losses. In response, heavier applications of chemical pesticides and new, more potent chemical pesticides are being used to control these pests. Hazardous chemicals are showing up at higher levels

Figure 1.1 In a world where biotechnology is used responsibly, scientists predict that healthier and more abundant foods could be available. There could be cloned animals used for production of foods, medication, and other useful products. Better health care could be possible for more people, leading to less suffering and longer life expectancies.

in the environment. These chemicals are being blamed for many immune and behavioral disorders. No cures for degenerative brain diseases have been found, but the number of people with these diseases is increasing. It is speculated that these increases result from the spread of **prion** diseases as well as unidentified environmental factors. Increased numbers of **emerging diseases** have spread like wildfire through both modern industrialized countries and developing countries. There is still no cure for AIDS, cancer, **Lyme disease**, **Ebola virus**, **tuberculosis**, and a number of newly emerged and reemerging diseases. Heart disease and obesity remain the leading causes of premature death in wealthy countries, while infectious disease and famine are the leading causes of death in other parts of the world.

A third possibility can also be imagined and considered, a world where biotechnology has taken a bad turn. Ethical discussions have been suppressed or ignored in favor of an unrestricted free-market economy. Few laws have been enacted to prevent groups with selfish interests either from misusing biotechnology that has potential risks to society or from conducting morally questionable experiments. Opponents of biotechnology see their worst fears being realized. Private interests have pursued every imaginable avenue to maximize the profits from this technology while completely disregarding public safety or welfare. All sensible laws and regulations designed to protect the interest of the public have been suppressed or ignored so there are no impediments to the pursuit of profit.

In this world, there are strange, never-before-seen plant and animal mutants. Some have escaped into the environment and are out-competing natural plants and animals. Some of the plants produce powerful drugs that can have serious side effects on an animal or person who might mistakenly ingest them. **Infertile** fish that have been engineered to grow larger than wild fish are preferentially mating with the wild fish. As a result of these non-productive matings, fewer fish are being born in the wild, causing populations of important natural **fisheries** to rapidly decline. No regulations protect these wild fish.

Because there are no guidelines about genetically engineering children, wealthy parents who can afford the expensive therapies have the option of genetically enhancing their children. The poor cannot afford this option. These genetically enhanced children are more intelligent, taller, stronger, and more athletic, and they can even live longer. These "superior" individuals have begun to discriminate against the "natural born."

There are now cures for virtually every possible medical condition, but again, only the rich can afford most of these. Many families of modest income become bankrupt trying to pay for a cure if someone in their family becomes seriously ill. Without laws regulating health insurance, insurance companies have no incentives to pay for these very expensive treatments. Everyone's genetic profile is stored in government files and any insurance company, employer, or government official has full access to that information. This genetic information is used to decide whether or not to insure individuals and what premium level to charge them. It is used to select employees based on their genetic probability of succeeding at a particular job and to discriminate against people with traits viewed as undesirable by one group or another.

Terrorists have been able to get access to dangerous **pathogens**. They have learned to use the technology needed to weaponize these agents. The world must be on constant alert to protect the public from their attacks. In one lab, a shortsighted researcher has combined two highly pathogenic viruses to create a "super" virus. Once this virus enters a host, the host dies within a day. It is 95% lethal and spreads very quickly from host to host. There is no known vaccine or cure. This researcher works for an unregulated company that specializes in creating new organisms that have applications as **bioweapons**. The researcher decides to mail a sample of the virus to a colleague across the country. There are no laws that forbid this.

The package is accidentally damaged. The workers who clean up the mess get sick and go home to their families. The next day they are all rushed to the hospital but soon all are dead.

Each of these three worlds is a caricature of what might be possible in our future. There are aspects of each that we must consider and understand. Let's first ask ourselves, "What kind of future do we want?" It is up to thoughtful, informed citizens to help shape the future in ways that make sense. We can use the practice of ethical debate to distinguish behavior that society judges to be "good" from that which is "bad." The best future achieved using biotechnology will come from applying appropriate, thoughtful, sensible laws and regulations that limit and guide the field, yet also provide flexibility for discoveries in new directions.

There are many reasons why new laws are being created to address advances in biotechnology. Biotechnology is a very powerful technology with the potential to transform our lives entirely. But it is in our best interest as a society that this transformation happens in ways that lead to the greatest benefit. In the past, technologies seemed simply to burst into our world and our awareness. Little public forethought was given to the impact of these new technologies. Both the positive benefits and the negative consequences of these technologies occurred, and people had to learn to adjust and compensate. For instance, the birth of the nuclear age occurred in this way. The technology was largely developed in secrecy during World War II. The public only became widely aware of the technology when the first atom bombs were dropped on Japan. Later, fear of using the technology helped fuel the Cold War between the United States and the former Soviet Union. For nearly 30 years, the two countries carried on an arms race to outdo one another's nuclear arsenal, at a tremendous expense to both countries. Growing up in the 1950s and 1960s meant practicing for a sudden nuclear attack while at school. In the end, the financial drain on the Soviet economy from this arms race led to the fall of the Soviet Union and the end of the Nuclear Arms Race.

Stop and Consider

How does biotechnology affect your life? Remember that biotechnology is any technology that uses living systems to create a useful product. This includes cooking, farming, medicine, and manufacturing.

How will biotechnology affect the future? Many authorities predict that the next great transition in our society and the world will be based on the introduction of biotechnology into our lives. The impact on our lives will rival or surpass the impact of the introduction of computers. Of course, no one is certain, but computer technology may provide a good example of how dramatic the transition could be. So again, imagine what the world would be like without computers. There would be no e-mail, just "snail mail," no Internet or World Wide Web, no word processing, no computer graphics or artwork, no computer games, no instant messenger. Twenty years ago people were asking questions about how the world would change if every home had a computer, and few people believed it would happen. Computers were too expensive, too exotic, too complicated for just anyone to use. Yet is that not exactly what has happened in the last 20 years? Computers have become an integral part of almost everyone's life. For many, it would be difficult, if not impossible, to carry on from day to day if computers all suddenly stopped working. Young people today have grown up with computers everywhere: at home, at school, in the library, even in coffee shops. There is an almost instinctive acceptance of their place in our day-to-day life. Computers have transformed the world, and today they impact nearly every aspect of our lives (Figure 1.2).

Figure 1.2 Computers have become an integral part of our lives. They are found in the classroom as a learning tool and even in cafés where we go to eat and relax.

Considering the potential impact biotechnology could have on our lives and the world, it is our responsibility as good citizens to help form public policy concerning how this technology should and should not be used. This is actually a revolutionary idea, too. When nuclear power was unleashed on the world, there was little public debate and few laws regulating its use. Later, when issues about its safety emerged, laws and regulations were introduced. Now there are so many laws and regulations in this country that it takes both the Nuclear Regulatory Commission and the Department of Defense to administer them (Figure 1.3). As computers were developed

Figure 1.3 Nuclear power is one form of technology that is carefully regulated.

and became widely available, few laws restricted their distribution and use. Now, privacy laws protect computer communications and copyright laws apply to computer software; there are laws addressing spam and Internet usage. These technologies came first, as is true with many other technologies. Only later were laws introduced to regulate these technologies. However, biotechnology is unique in the degree to which people are passionate in their attitudes toward this technology. Its ability to transform life makes it a very powerful tool. It frightens some people and excites others. However, virtually everyone familiar with the technology believes that the human race needs to make proper use of this technology to better our world, not harm it. To accomplish this, we need strong and clear ideas of what we believe are ethical and unethical ways to use this technology. Laws based on our ethical judgments will be needed to help protect those who invest their time and wealth into bringing this technology to its full potential. And laws will be needed to protect the public from those who would use this technology to exploit others. Laws will be needed to protect the environment in some cases, and in other cases to limit the uses of the technology.

A discussion of current ethical opinions addressing important new developments in biotechnology follows in the chapters of this book. This book was written to help you form your own opinions and ideas about how this technology should and should not be used. It is critical that all of us decide what we believe is just and moral concerning the use of biotechnology and that we make our views known to those around us. In this way, we can influence what future world we will live in.

Stop and Consider

Do any biotechnology issues worry you? Which ones? Why?

CONNECTIONS

Many forces are already at work changing our world. In the next few decades, biotechnology is likely to be one of the most powerful technologies. As this technology is developed, people will often try to shape our views about biotechnology in order to influence if and how it is used. As informed citizens, if we do not help make those decisions, they will be made for us by others who may not necessarily have our best interests in mind. We can participate in the decision process in many ways. One way to participate is to continue reading this book so as to better understand some of the complex issues biotechnology poses for humanity. Another way to participate is to stay informed about new technological advances and controversies, and then make your voice heard by as many people as you can influence. Make a difference; this is your world to have or to lose. And always be sure to vote!

FOR MORE INFORMATION

For more information about the concepts discussed in this chapter, search the Web using the following keywords:

Biotechnology, **Genetic engineering**, **The Cold War**, **Biotechnology and ethics**, **Bioethics**

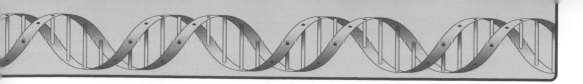

2

Why Think
About Ethics?

BASIC CONCEPTS IN ETHICS

"How should we live?" That is the big question addressed by the field
of **ethics**. Simply stated, ethics is the science and philosophy of
morality. Morality is a "code of behavior" defined by society through
law, religion, or philosophy. This code of behavior is largely influenced by a society's social, political, and economic environment.

When discussing ethics, it is helpful to keep in mind basic
assumptions about the type of morality being discussed. One view,
called moral relativism, states that morality is not necessarily
defined in the same way for everyone all the time. Morality may be
different in different societies, or it may change over time as a society evolves. This means that what is ethical for one group may not
necessarily be considered ethical by another, leading to conflicting
ideas of what is moral. In this view, morality is not static, but
evolves as societies change. In different circumstances, two people

can have conflicting behaviors that are considered moral by their own group. Human conditions have changed dramatically over the past centuries and so the moral relativistic view of ethics can adapt to this change. Understanding this can lead to tolerance of diverse views.

Objectivism is another view of morality, which states that universal moral principles exist for all people. This view broadly refers to the range of behaviors that are acceptable to "all rational persons" regardless of where or when they live. It holds that, in any group of reasonable people, a set of behaviors can be defined that are considered good and bad. For example, the killing of another human is immoral (bad) and feeding the hungry is moral (good) (Figure 2.1).

Keeping in mind how relativism and objectivism affect peoples' thinking about morality, we can discuss, understand, and decide what we believe to be moral behavior. This task is very important for us as individuals and for humanity if we are to avoid misunderstandings and conflict. In daily life, we are faced with many moral choices. Ethics helps us know how to make the right choice, the moral choice, as well as how to understand and participate in a dialogue with those whose views we disagree with or whose views disagree with our own.

Because humans are highly social, it is critical that we get along with each other if we are to thrive and coexist in peace. It is in our best interest to cooperate to achieve the wonderfully complex relationships we develop in our families, communities, states, nations, and the world. People living in a group will naturally define what is fair in their interactions with one another. These concepts of fairness evolve into the moral code of behavior. The code may be unspoken, or it may be defined in laws, regulations, philosophy, religious beliefs, or commandments. A well-known example is The Golden Rule, which states: "We should do to others what we would want others to do to us." Once a code is established in a society, means of enforcement are developed. Gossip is an informal but very

Figure 2.1 Feeding the less fortunate is considered a moral act. The people in this photograph are distributing Thanksgiving meals to those who do not have enough to eat.

powerful example of how this code is enforced. If someone's behavior is outside acceptable limits, then members of the community will begin to talk about the person's behavior, with the intent of pressuring the individual to return to living by the acceptable moral code. Laws and religious practices are other ways that we enforce a code of moral behaviors.

The Greeks, and later the Romans, are credited with first formally studying ethics. Socrates, Plato, and Aristotle are among the earliest known ethicists (Figure 2.2). They used ethics to debate and understand moral behaviors. Other groups known for their interest in ethics include ancient Hindus, Jews, Christians, Jains,

Figure 2.2 Plato was one of the early philosophers who proposed theories on ethics and morals. In this painting, Plato is seen conversing with a student at a Greek academy.

entitled. We must honor those rights. Our society considers life, liberty, and the pursuit of happiness to be basic rights. These rights include the right to own property, the right of religious expression, the right of freedom of speech, and the right of free movement. These rights are considered universal and apply to all people equally. We are born with these rights and they are inalienable, meaning one cannot give them up or decide one does not want them any longer. These rights are the foundation of America's freedom.

Stop and Consider

Many influences in our lives help us formulate our moral values. These include religious as well as nonreligious sources. Where have you learned your moral values? What are some important moral values that you have learned and who taught these to you?

Finally, by examining the consequences of our actions, we can determine whether or not our behavior is moral. If our actions result in outcomes that are more favorable than unfavorable, then they can be considered moral. However, there are some cases that are illustrated by the saying, "The ends justify the means," where someone may try to justify immoral behavior by claiming that there will ultimately be a favorable outcome for an individual or for a group of people. There may be a claim that the good outweighs the harm. In these cases, other moral criteria need to be applied to ensure that people are not harmed.

APPLIED ETHICS

Applied ethics is a branch of ethics used to analyze specific moral issues such as gun control, physician-assisted suicide, capital punishment, and many other topics discussed in this book. But for a given issue to become a moral issue, it must meet certain criteria. It must first be controversial to a significant number of people who are divided for and against the issue. To say that murder is an applied ethical issue is inaccurate, because all reasonable people can agree that murder is wrong. However, physician-assisted suicide, where a doctor is called in to help someone who chooses to end his or her life due to illness or old age, is an applied ethical issue because there are reasonable people for and against this action. The second criterion is that the issue must be distinctly moral and not just a heated topic of social disagreement. For example, we have social policies or laws about traffic speed. There is considerable disagreement about how fast we should be allowed to drive on a given road. Those who live in a particular neighborhood generally want traffic to slow down, while those who need to get to work on time when they are late want to drive faster. Though this is an important issue and people may have heated discussions about the appropriate speed, this is not a moral issue but rather an issue of social policy. However, if we ask the question, "Is it alright to break an established law?" then the discussion becomes a question of morality and can be addressed by ethics. Social and moral issues often overlap, but ethics is only properly used when examining issues of morality.

In using applied ethics to debate an issue of morality, it is important to address the virtues, duties, and consequences related to an issue that people on both sides of the issue agree have merit. Virtues provide a set of premises that grant a moral foundation to the debate. Duties provide a list of principles that guide our actions toward others. These principles may include benevolence, honesty, and recognition of another person's rights. Examining consequences establishes whether or not personal and social benefits are associated with an issue. Applied ethics provides a means to understand the questions of morality that an issue raises and to look for common ground upon which people on both sides of the issue can agree. We can use applied ethics to decide what is moral, both on a personal and on a social level. Assuming that we all think it is best to live in a moral society, this becomes the basis for creating morally correct positions that can be adopted by society. In this book, we will examine ethics related to biotechnology. Throughout this book, we will consider questions that arise from using this method of analyzing morality so that we can explore whether or not we believe these new technologies should be permitted.

BIOETHICS

In the 1950s and 1960s, physicians and theologians came together to discuss difficult questions arising from medical advances of the time. Some of these questions were about using human subjects in research, some were about the use of new medical technologies, and some were about protecting the public from harmful medications. The outcome was the beginning of modern bioethics. The term *bioethics* was first introduced and discussed in 1971 by Van Rensselaer Potter, a Professor of Oncology at the University of Wisconsin. At that time, the term *bioethics* referred to ethics related to the survival and the improvement of human life. However, today, because of the accelerating rate of new discoveries that are creating increasingly complex and urgent ethical issues, the term is used to refer to broader issues in medicine and bioscience. In current usage, the term *bioethics* can include topics in biology, biotechnology, medicine, environment, population control, and ecology. The topics presented in this book are all important topics in the public's bioethical debates, as are virtually any discussions related to acceptable usages of biotechnology. The discussion of bioethics in this book, however, will be limited to only a few of the many remarkable scientific breakthroughs of the past decade.

Modern bioethics

A notable aspect of bioethical discussions today is that much of the debate is occurring before discoveries are being made or technologies are becoming available for widespread use. This does not generally happen when new technologies are discovered and introduced to the public. In the past, as is generally true today, new technologies are introduced to the public after they have been developed and are ready for use. People, over time, learn about any positive or negative fallout from the technology. Generally, ethical debates begin only if there are apparent reasons for concern. The public is not generally consulted by those introducing new technologies. The public isn't considered to have the background or interest to make decisions about whether or not a new technology should be used. An example of this occurred when people around the world began to understand the degree of devastation of civilians that resulted when secret nuclear weapons were exploded on Japan in 1945. Decades of ethical debate followed concerning the use of nuclear technology, which helped to fuel the Cold War and has led to our current public position of reluctance and mistrust of nuclear technology. However, this is not the pattern being practiced in modern bioethics.

An example is the Human Genome Project (HGP), the international effort to sequence the entire human genome, all 3 billion bases. The genetic information we inherit from our parents is encoded by **DNA** (**deoxyribonucleic acid**), which forms the 46 chromosomes found in the nucleus of the cells of our body. The DNA carries in its sequence of four bases, A, T, C and G, instructions for the 30,000 or so genes that instruct our cells how to make the proteins needed to create all the cells, tissues, and organs of our body. The Human Genome Project, started in the mid 1980s by the U.S. Department of Energy and the National Institutes of Health, developed into an international project in laboratories around the world, drawing on the skill, expertise, and hard work of thousands of scientists.

Today, bioethical issues arising from the HGP are carefully studied by many organizations including the federally funded Ethical, Legal, and Social Implications Research Program (ELSI). This organization was started by Dr. James Watson, the first director of the Human Genome Project. Watson realized the unprecedented nature of the knowledge that humankind was about to acquire by learning the nucleotide sequence of the entire human genome. In his position as director of the HGP, he arranged to set aside 3% of the project's budget to explore ethical, legal, and social implications of the HGP. Later, Senator Al Gore of Tennessee raised this amount to 5%. As the HGP progressed over the years toward its goal of sequencing the human genome, ELSI funded many initiatives around the country, including public debate and education, to help prepare humanity for the impact of this new knowledge and technology. These efforts are helping to ensure that humanity benefits and is not harmed by the powerful discoveries arising from the HGP.

Holding an ethical debate about the use of a new technology before the technology has been used is challenging because those participating in the debate can only speculate about the probable outcomes since there is no way to see into the future and find out the actual outcomes. These speculative debates are further

The Human Genome Project

The Human Genome Project is a worldwide research effort that succeeded in determining the entire nucleotide sequence of the 23 pairs of human chromosomes. In 2003, the nearly complete nucleotide sequence of the human genome was published so that scientists around the world would have access to the information.

Each of our chromosomes is a long strand of nucleotides. These strands can be many millions of nucleotides long. Within our 23 pairs of chromosomes there are an estimated 3 billion nucleotides. It is the order of these nucleotides that stores the genetic information necessary for human life. The Human Genome Project took 13 years to decipher the order of these nucleotides. Now scientists can look at this information and begin to learn how information is coded and stored in our DNA. With this under-standing will come new opportunities to find medical cures and new biotechnologies to better our lives.

complicated when people hold ideas that are biased by their own misunderstanding or lack of understanding of how the technology works.

In the debate on human cloning, for example, there are those who misunderstand the process of cloning and believe that cloning can be used to make exact duplicates of a person down to the last freckle. In this view, a human clone would have the same personality, age, and perhaps even the same memories as its donor. This type of cloning is only seen in science fiction; it is not what is meant when scientists speak of human cloning. The actual processes used to clone an organism and the real outcomes are covered in Chapters 3 and 4. However, to clarify what could be accomplished with human cloning, if someone ever tries, these cloned humans would have to go through all the stages of development that any normally conceived human would experience. This means that all of the unique circumstances that a clone will encounter during its growth and development will ensure that it becomes different and distinct from its donor. With the same genes, the clone and its donor are likely to have similar outward appearances as well as some other similar physical and personality traits. However, due to the extensive influence exerted by the environment on an organism's development, a clone and a donor would also have many differences.

There is thus a danger that people who have misconceptions about what is achievable through human cloning may arrive at a very different moral judgment than they would if they understood what the technology is actually likely to achieve. This may lead to false conclusions that may end up delaying beneficial technologies or, conversely, to permit the use of harmful technologies. In these cases, it is important to educate the public so that, to the greatest possible degree, the public understands the technology and can formulate informed opinions.

PAST BIOETHICAL ISSUES

The drama and controversy surrounding the first **recombinant DNA** experiments provide a good example of how the scientific community addressed a potentially dangerous new technology. In 1975, 140 scientists from around the world gathered for the now famous Asilomar Conference on Recombinant DNA held in Pacific Grove, California. The conference was organized by the scientists to discuss the safety of recombinant DNA technology. The concern leading to the conference began in 1973 when two scientists, Herbert Boyer, a biochemist at the University of California at San Francisco, and Stanley Cohen, an associate professor of medicine at Stanford University, became the world's first genetic engineers. They reported that they had succeeded in combining the DNA from different organisms, thereby creating the first recombinant DNA molecule. They introduced their recombinant molecules into bacteria and were able to "clone" the recombinant DNA. This means that they used bacteria to produce vast numbers of copies of their recombinant DNA constructs. They first combined two bacterial **plasmids** containing different antibiotic-resistant genes and later they combined DNA from a frog with bacterial DNA. The discovery of this technology meant that scientists would one day be able to select any gene of interest and move it into another organism to have it expressed (Figure 2.3). One of the very first uses of this technology was to express the human insulin gene in bacteria. Later, Genentech, the world's first biotechnology company, started by Herbert Boyer, used this technology to produce large amounts of insulin in bacteria for the treatment of diabetes.

When the scientific community first heard of recombinant DNA technology, there was enormous excitement, but there was also an underlying unease. One source of the scientists' concern was the suggestion that a team of scientists was planning to use the technique to put genetic material from a virus that

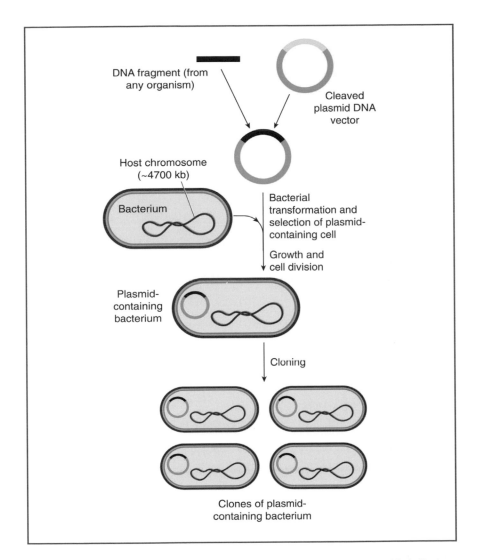

Figure 2.3 Recombinant DNA is DNA that has been created artificially by isolating a gene from one organism and inserting it into a semicircular piece of DNA called a plasmid, which is found in bacteria. This plasmid serves as a vector through which the isolated gene's DNA can be inserted into a host bacterium. The DNA is then duplicated in large quantities as the bacterial host multiplies. The protein from these clones can be removed from their hosts and used to create a variety of genetically engineered products.

causes cancer in mice into bacteria that is normally found in our stomachs. No one knew whether or not this virus would cause cancer in humans and the idea that a common bacterium might accidentally infect many people and cause cancer was quite alarming. It was clear to many of these scientists that they needed to develop a set of rules or guidelines for this new technology, or not only would people be put at risk, but also public fear would lead to a government prohibition on recombinant DNA research. In response, Paul Berg, a Professor of Biochemistry at Stanford University School of Medicine whose ingenious research helped pave the way for recombinant DNA technology, organized a worldwide moratorium for all recombinant DNA experiments. Many scientists believed that research on recombinant DNA technology should not continue until safety concerns and adequate containment techniques had been developed. Since the technology was so new, there were fears about using the technology. Fears like the risk of inadvertently releasing cloned cancer-causing genes into the environment and causing wide-spread disease or worse.

At the 1975 Asilomar Conference, recommendations were published addressing the safe handling and disposal of recombinant DNA molecules, the types of organisms to be used to clone these molecules, and the types of experiments that were judged safe to conduct. Later, these recommendations were used by the National Institutes of Health (NIH) to establish a list of safety guidelines for conducting recombinant DNA research. The guidelines were viewed by the scientific community as a way to ensure that the technology was safe before it was widely used.

It was felt by some scientists that the guidelines were unnec-essarily restrictive and would hamper research progress. Other scientists, as well as non-scientists following the debate, felt the recommendations were not restrictive enough to protect the public. After all, they reasoned, this was a new and not well understood manipulation of the basic building blocks of life. The town of Cambridge, Massachusetts, where both Harvard University and the Massachusetts Institute of Technology are located, instituted a town-wide ban on all recombinant DNA research to the great disappointment of the scientists at both of these institutions. While the result of this ban, and other actions around the country, severely limited the progress of recombinant DNA research, scientists supported the measures and agreed to follow the guidelines. It wasn't long before measures such as the Cambridge ban were dropped when it became apparent that the NIH guidelines were working to ensure public safety.

In 1979, with more experience and knowledge, the Recombinant DNA Advisory Committee (RAC) at the NIH felt comfortable enough to establish much less restrictive guidelines. As a result, during the next few decades, recombinant DNA research was largely viewed as safe. Since then, recombinant DNA research has become so commonplace that it is now routinely carried out in high school biology classes. Many students conduct experiments such as inserting the green fluorescent protein from jellyfish into *E. coli*, which causes the bacteria cells to fluoresce under UV light.

Such careful consideration before using a powerful new technology is a good example of bioethics in action. As stated, many scientists were unhappy about the restrictive guidelines that were adopted at the 1975 Asilomar Conference. They felt that research with great potential to help humanity was being needlessly delayed. Others were unhappy with the loss of opportunities to use the technology to develop marketable products and make a profit. However, it is a credit to these scientists that they acted ethically and worked within the guidelines until it was determined by the scientific community and government agencies, such as the NIH, that the technology would not cause widespread harm. After the first NIH Guidelines on recombinant DNA research were developed and the moratorium was lifted, scientists could only receive

NIH funds for recombinant DNA work if they and their institution provided assurance that they would work within the Guidelines and had the skill, knowledge, and equipment to do so. As experience has shown that the technology would not cause widespread harm, the NIH Guidelines on recombinant DNA work have become less restrictive, except for work with very dangerous disease-causing agents such as the human immunodeficiency virus (HIV) and the Ebola virus.

CONNECTIONS

The debate surrounding recombinant DNA technology is a good example of how ethics must play a role in helping scientists and the public determine acceptable and unacceptable ways to pursue research. This chapter began by asking the question, "How should we live?" It is the intent of ethics to help us answer that question. Nothing is more gratifying than to review one's life and feel proud that one is living morally. Many people can claim this to be true, but many people cannot.

Discussions about ethics and morality become rather complex and, at times, hard to follow. It is a fascinating topic that many great thinkers have pondered. The dawn of modern biotechnology provided an example of society, specifically the practitioners of the early science, coming together to debate and discuss how to proceed in a way that protects society, but does not hamper inquiry. It is important to understand that one does not have to understand all the complexities of the great thinkers' arguments or be a scientist on the cutting edge of a new technology to come to one's own conclusions about ethical ways to function. For each topic covered in this book, there are many justifiable views. Remember to pay attention to your thought process as you explore these topics, so that when you are finished reading, you will be able to come to your own conclusions about the morality of using these new advances in biotechnology that could change our way of life.

FOR MORE INFORMATION

For more information about the concepts discussed in this chapter, search the Web using the following keywords:

Applied ethics, Human Genome Project, Ethical, Legal, and Social Implications Research Program (ELSI), Recombinant DNA, Asilomar Conference, National Institutes of Health

3

A Brave New World of Clones

SHOULD THE CLONING OF ANIMALS AND HUMANS BE PERMITTED?
One of the most debated ethical questions of our time is whether
or not humans or other animals should be cloned. The question
of human cloning is especially complex because it asks us to
examine what makes us special as humans. Would a clone be
somehow less than human? How could that be? After all, is it not
true that any human being, no matter what that person's origins,
is still human? But perhaps the answer is linked to why the clone
would be created: To replace a loved one? To serve as an organ
donor? To create a cloned army or a workforce of slaves? Would
the clone be "required" to fulfill the role for which it was created?
What if the clone does not want to be a loved one, an organ donor,
or a cloned soldier? Who gets to choose?

Human cloning and animal cloning have many commonalities,
including the technology used in the cloning procedures and with

some of the ethical issues that arise. It is therefore sometimes hard to discuss one without reference to the other. However, ethical questions specific to human cloning will be addressed in more detail in the next chapter. This chapter will discuss the scientific basis of cloning and focus on ethical questions surrounding the cloning of animals. This issue is somewhat less controversial than human cloning, but it nonetheless presents very important ethical issues.

WHAT IS A CLONE?

In biology, the term *clone* is defined and used in several ways, a fact which can confuse the discussion. To complicate matters further, the term is often used differently in public discussion. To discuss the ethics of cloning, it is necessary to accurately define what is meant by cloning and to eliminate confusion. One definition of a clone is an exact **genetic** copy of a cell or an organism. DNA molecules that are exact copies of an original DNA molecule can also be clones. "Clone" can also be used as a verb to mean the act of creating a cloned cell, organism, or molecule. The original meaning of the word *clone* (*klon* in Greek) is "twig." This meaning arose because it is possible to create many types of plants by taking a cutting or "twig" from a parent plant and rooting these cuttings. A rooted cutting will then grow into a new plant. This new plant is a genetic clone of the parent plant because it has all of the exact same genes as the parent plant. However, while these cloned plants share many identical traits with the parent plant and have the exact same genetic information, they will not resemble one another in every way. While they are genetic clones, the plants will be different sizes and have their own branching patterns and distinct look. In this situation, the plants would still be clones though they have different appearances. So, clones may or may not look exactly alike.

Many types of cells from **eukaryotic** organisms can be cloned by isolating a single cell and growing it in culture. These cells reproduce by simple cell division, called **mitosis**. Since there is no mixing of genes between cells during mitosis, the resulting **daughter cells** (offspring) are all genetically identical (Figure 3.1). This creates a population of cloned cells, called a cell line. Because these cells are all genetically identical, they are also clones, though they may also not all look alike.

Cloned cells and cloned organisms are created asexually. In other words, only one parent transmits genetic information to the offspring. Most animals reproduce sexually, with two parents contributing genetic material. This ensures a mixing of genes that always results in offspring genetically distinct from either parent. The mixing of genes from a mother and father in sexual repro- duction is an important survival mechanism for a species because it creates **genetic diversity**. Genetic diversity means that there is variability within any given species for any given trait that may make some individuals more fit to survive than others. These more fit individuals help assure the survival of the species during stressful times. But clones are genetically identical to their single parent, which eliminates the possibility of genetic diversity and so is viewed by some as limiting a species' chances to survive.

Some people believe that cloning is like photocopying an organism. In a way this is true, but only the **genotype** (all the genes of an organism) of the clone is the same as that of the parental or "donor" organism. In other words, clone and parent have the same DNA and therefore the same genes. A clone is not, however, an exact duplicate of an adult organism in other respects. It is beyond our scientific capabilities to create an exact duplicate of any adult organism, because an individual organism is much more than the sum of its genes. Creating exact duplicates of an organism is only possible in science fiction.

Clones are also not created as fully formed adult organisms. All clones must go through the normal stages of development to reach maturity. For humans, this includes time as an embryo, a fetus,

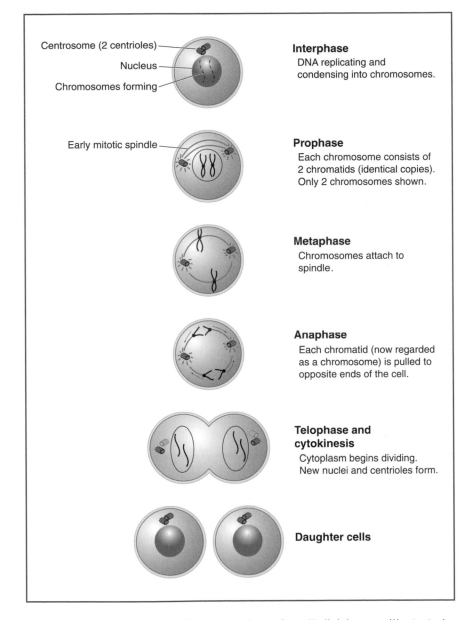

Centrosome (2 centrioles)

Nucleus

Chromosomes forming

Interphase
DNA replicating and
condensing into chromosomes.

Early mitotic spindle

Prophase
Each chromosome consists of
2 chromatids (identical copies).
Only 2 chromosomes shown.

Metaphase
Chromosomes attach to
spindle.

Anaphase
Each chromatid (now regarded
as a chromosome) is pulled to
opposite ends of the cell.

**Telophase and
cytokinesis**
Cytoplasm begins dividing.
New nuclei and centrioles form.

Daughter cells

Figure 3.1 The stages of mitosis in eukaryotic cell division are illustrated here. The daughter cells produced by mitosis have the same genetic information and are considered genetic clones when grown in culture.

an infant, a child, and an adult. The clone's memories and experiences during this period of growth will be unique and therefore will make the clone a unique individual, even if it looks just like the donor organism. This takes time, and while this time is passing, the parent is also aging and changing, making the donor and clone even more different from one another. In addition, the lifetime experiences of an organism are not recorded in its genes and cannot be transmitted from donor to clone via information stored in DNA. Thus, it is not feasible to clone a human or any organism with the same memories and personality as an already existing adult organism.

There are other reasons why clones are not photocopies. An organism's genes only partially determine how an organism grows and develops. The environment in which the organism develops strongly influences how it grows and ultimately turns out. Scientists still debate to what extent an organism's genes versus the environment contributes to a grown organism's individuality. This debate is often called "*Nature vs. Nurture*".

Those who believe that nature is the stronger influence hold the idea that living things are primarily a product of our genetic makeup. They believe that genes largely determine how an organism develops and what it ultimately becomes. In this view, the environment plays only a small role in influencing the outcome. In certain human traits, a strong genetic influence is easily observed and supports the point of view that nature plays the greater role. Traits such as eye color, hair color, and skin color are determined largely by genetic factors. We generally resemble our parents with regard to these traits which are inherited and determined mostly by the genes we receive.

On the other side of the "Nature vs. Nurture" debate are people who strongly believe that the environment has a greater influence on how an organism ultimately turns out. In this view, "nurture" has the stronger influence. For instance, people who live in an environment with access to a complete and nutritious diet tend to be noticeably taller and healthier than people who have a deficient diet. In this example, diet is considered an environmental factor that influences the way genes are used by an organism. In this case, environmental factors such as diet have a more pronounced influence than genetic factors on how tall or healthy an individual is. Most scientists now believe that both genetics and environment have strong influences on an organism's growth and development.

Another reason that a clone will not turn out to be an exact duplicate of the parent who donated the genes has to do with the unique qualities of the egg or **ovum** used in the cloning process. Each ovum is harvested from a separate donor who is almost always a different individual than the genetic donor, who is providing only the nucleus and genes used in the cloning process. Though this may only lead to subtle differences, the environment within the egg used for cloning needs to be considered. First, the egg will provide some of the clone's DNA in the form of **mitochondrial DNA**. While mitochondrial DNA makes up only a small portion of the total cellular DNA, the mitochondrial genes do play an import role in the cell's **energy metabolism**. Second, the proteins and other molecules of any given egg interact with the genes of the donor nucleus in subtly different ways that scientists do not yet fully understand. To illustrate how different eggs can interact with the same DNA to produce slightly different outcomes, imagine going into a television store and looking at all of the TV sets. Often, they are all showing the same program because they are all receiving the same signal. Yet each TV set has its own subtly unique version of the picture, with slight differences in color, sound quality, and sharpness of the image. Similarly, the donor egg leaves its own subtle but unique contribution, making every clone unique and different from its genetic donor.

Perhaps in some far distant future, science may permit us to duplicate an existing organism molecule by molecule. Then we may be able to make clones that are an exact "photocopy" of the original, but this is not what is being done today in laboratories. Today when we use the term *clone,* it only means that the donor and the clone share most of the same genetic information used for growth and development.

PAST AND PRESENT EFFORTS TO CLONE ANIMALS

Animal cloning is considered to have begun with the experiments that the German scientist Hans Spemann conducted on salamander embryos early in the 20th century. He used very fine baby's hair tied around a single fertilized egg cell to split the egg in two. He found that sometimes one or both of these split egg cells developed into whole organisms, thus forming cloned salamanders (Figure 3.2). Today, this form of cloning is referred to as twinning because it is a way to experimentally create identical twin organisms. Since identical twins have the exact same DNA, they are also genetic clones. Later, in the 1950s, Robert Briggs and Thomas J. King, at the Institute for Cancer Research in Philadelphia, produced the first cloned frogs using nuclear transfer protocols that they developed. They removed the nucleus from leopard frog eggs and inserted a nuclei from developing embryo cells. Three decades later, this same feat was accomplished using mammalian egg cells. This delay was partially due to the much smaller size of mammalian eggs. The first cloned mammals were created in the 1980s. These included rabbits, pigs, mice, cows, and monkeys. But these early clones were derived from embryonic cells, not adult cells. Based on earlier work, scientists believed that it might not be possible to use adult cells to clone an animal. Then in 1996, Ian Wilmut and Keith Campbell, at the Roslin Institute in Edinburgh, Scotland, announced the birth of Dolly the sheep. Dolly's birth marked the first time a mammal was cloned from an adult cell (Figure 3.3). Wilmut and Campbell's breakthrough with Dolly ignited a worldwide debate about whether or not cloning

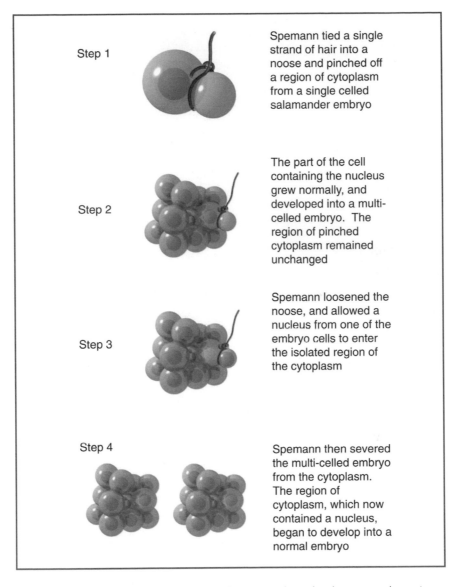

Step 1

Spemann tied a single strand of hair into a noose and pinched off a region of cytoplasm from a single celled salamander embryo

Step 2

The part of the cell containing the nucleus grew normally, and developed into a multi-celled embryo. The region of pinched cytoplasm remained unchanged

Step 3

Spemann loosened the noose, and allowed a nucleus from one of the embryo cells to enter the isolated region of the cytoplasm

Step 4

Spemann then severed the multi-celled embryo from the cytoplasm. The region of cytoplasm, which now contained a nucleus, began to develop into a normal embryo

Figure 3.2 The steps involved in Spemann's twinning experiments are illustrated here. Spemann took a fertilized salamander egg and tied it off with a strand of hair. This caused the egg to develop into a multi-celled embryo.

Figure 3.3 Dolly (1996–2003) the cloned sheep was the first mammal to be cloned from adult cells. This was accomplished by Ian Wilmut and Keith Campbell at the Roslin Institute in Scotland. Dolly is photographed here, being fed by Ian Wilmut.

was moral and whether or not it should be legal because, for the first time, it was demonstrated that cells from an adult animal could be used to clone genetic copies of an adult. Some people became concerned that this capability could be misused to exploit cloned organisms, including cloned humans. These concerns will be covered later in this chapter and in the next chapter as they relate to human cloning.

After the cloning of Dolly, other mammals were successfully cloned from adult cells, including mice, rabbits, goats, cows, pigs, and cats. Many people believe human cloning may one day be feasible because of these successes. But before any human cloning is attempted, successful cloning of other closely related primates must be demonstrated. While monkey embryos have been successfully cloned from adult cells, none of these have so far resulted in live births. This is significant because humans, like monkeys, are primates. Until cloning of nonhuman primates is successful, most scientists feel human cloning should not be attempted under any circumstances because to do so would violate established medical ethics rules related to experimentation on human subjects.

HOW ANIMAL CLONING IS DONE

Animal cloning is done in two basic ways. One is referred to as **twinning** or embryo splitting; the other is **somatic cell nuclear transfer** (**SCNT**). Twinning is not generally what is thought of when cloning is discussed in the media. Twinning is similar to the technique Spemann used with the salamander experiments in which he split fertilized embryos using baby's hair to achieve multiple births. It is accomplished by manually separating cells in developing embryos. This technique can be used to achieve multiple births from one fertilized egg. The resulting organisms are twins as well as clones. A variation of this method is commonly used to clone desirable animals for agriculture. The method uses a fertilized egg that is allowed to go through only a few rounds of cell divisions. These cells are then separated from one another and permitted to continue dividing. Each of these separated cells now has the potential to become a whole organism. If enough embryo-derived cells can be grown in culture, many clones or twins can be created this way.

While twinning is commonly used in modern agriculture, SCNT is the most controversial method used to create the cloned animals. This is because it is only newly developed and it is also the most likely way that human cloning would be accomplished. SCNT involves removing the nucleus from an unfertilized egg cell obtained from a female donor. The nucleus is removed using a process called **microinjection.** While looking at the donor egg cell through a high-powered microscope, a technician uses a very fine glass needle to puncture the cell and suck out the nucleus. This creates an enucleated egg cell. A nucleus from a donor cell is then obtained by microinjection and injected into the enucleated egg. In some procedures, the entire donor cell is fused with the enucleated egg by electrical stimulation or chemical means. The egg cell with the foreign nucleus is then either stimulated with an electrical current or treated chemically to start cell division. Once the egg cell begins to divide, it can be implanted into the uterus of a **surrogate mother** (Figure 3.4).

While SCNT is currently the best method for creating clones, it is still not efficient or reliable. SCNT is a very complicated process with many challenging steps in which damage can be done to the donor eggs, nuclei, or embryos. Every step must succeed for the clone to be born healthy. To clone Dolly the sheep, 277 embryos had to be created by removing the sheep egg nuclei and fusing adult donor cells from mammary tissue. Harvesting egg cells from sheep and fusing these with adult sheep cells is a costly, laborious, and time-consuming process. Of these 277 embryos created by somatic cell nuclear transfer, only 29 were judged suitable for transfer into surrogate mother sheep. From all this effort, only Dolly survived. This is a success rate of 3.4% for the 29 embryos implanted and is much lower if all 277 of the original eggs are included in the count. This is a fairly typical success rate for SCNT cloning in most of the animals that have been cloned. For cats, it took 87 cloned embryos to produce one healthy cloned cat, a 1.6% success rate. Only in cattle have success rates for the birth of healthy clones been as high as 40%, for unknown reasons.

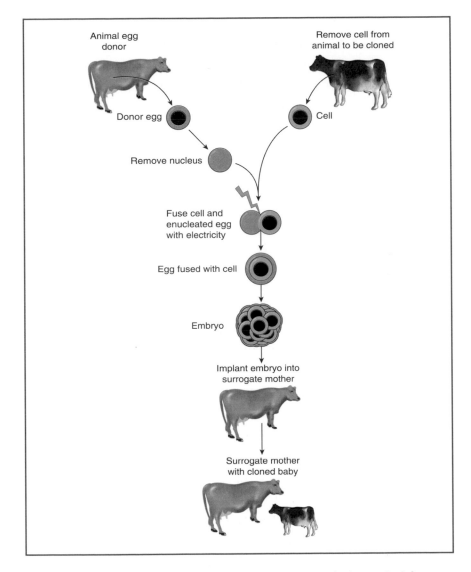

Figure 3.4 In SCNT (illustrated here), a donor egg is harvested from a female mammal. Using microinjection techniques, the nucleus is removed. Then the enucleated egg can be fused with an adult donor cell, or just the nucleus from a donor cell can be injected into the enucleated egg. The resulting cloned embryo is implanted into a surrogate mother where it develops into a cloned animal.

WHY CLONE AN ANIMAL?

Early scientists like Spemann were motivated to clone animals as a tool to help understand events in embryonic development. Spemann wanted to know what genetic and cellular changes occur as an organism develops from a single fertilized egg cell to a multicellular organism. Briggs and King wanted to learn whether embryonic and adult cells had the same genetic material or whether genetic information changed as the organism developed. Through their research, they learned that genetic information changes as cells differentiate into all the different cell types of an adult organism. They concluded that not all cells can be used in cloning and that embryonic cells were most effective. However, the exact nature of these genetic changes took years of research to discover and are still being explored.

It was Ian Wilmut and Keith Campbell who were the first scientists to succeed in finding a way to use adult cells for cloning when they successfully created Dolly. Wilmut and Campbell were able to develop a method to reprogram the genetic material in adult cells so that it could behave like DNA in a newly formed zygote. This process was very inefficient, but resulted in the birth of a living clone from the DNA of an adult cell.

Polly is another sheep cloned by the same scientists who cloned Dolly the sheep. Polly, however, was engineered to have a human gene for blood-clotting protein, known as **Factor IX**, expressed and secreted in her milk. Factor IX is used to treat **hemophilia** and other blood-clotting disorders. Producing Factor IX in her milk makes Polly a very valuable sheep. Scientists believe that they will be able to isolate and purify the clotting factor from Polly's milk. Originally, this drug was isolated from human plasma and could be contaminated with human infectious agents such as hepatitis or human immunodeficiency virus (HIV). Factor IX from Polly does not pose this risk, though there may be some sheep-specific infectious agents in her milk. Determining whether this is true is one reason the cloned Factor IX from sheep is not commercially available yet. Currently, Factor IX is isolated from genetically engineered animal cells that have the human gene for Factor IX. These cells are grown in large cultures and Factor IX can be isolated from the cells. If and when the cloned Factor IX from sheep milk is proven safe, then it may become a cheaper and more reliable source of this drug.

Other reasons animals are cloned are to create animals with desirable traits needed to improve agriculture, to conduct research, or to create better pets. Cows that produce the best meat or milk are being cloned to develop highly productive animals that one day might supply food. Someday, herds of cloned animals could have traits that could help them thrive in unfavorable climates, thereby bringing a food source to depressed regions of the world. Cloned mice and other lab animals have proven very useful in lab experiments because there is no genetic diversity to complicate the interpretation of experimental results. For example, two cloned mice that are genetically identical should have very similar life spans if kept in the same controlled environment. If one of these cloned mice receives an experimental treatment and the other control mouse doesn't receive the treatment and dies before the experimental treatment mouse, it is likely that the treatment, rather than possessing superior genes, is what kept the experimental mouse alive longer. Genetic superiority of one mouse over the other can thus be eliminated as a possible complication in interpreting the results of this experiment, making the conclusions more reliable.

People become very attached to their pets, and a pet's death can be very traumatic. The promise of being able to replace a lost pet with an identical copy can be a great enticement for some pet lovers. The first cloned cat was born in 2001 and named CC (short for "copycat"). CC was the first household pet to be cloned (Figure 3.5). Genetic Savings & Clone created CC and is

Figure 3.5 Lou Hawthorne, the CEO of Genetic Savings & Clone, is shown here with a picture of CC, the first cloned cat. Some people feel that cloning pets is an unethical use of biotechnology.

a company in the business of replacing lost pets with clones. In 2004, another cat, Little Nicky, was cloned to replace the original pet, named Nicky. This cloning service cost the pet owner $50,000. While cloning a pet cannot truly replace the lost pet because the experience and environment of the clone will influence its personality and behavior, cloned pets may turn out to be surprisingly similar to the originals. But the cloned pet will always be a unique animal. The cloned animal may even turn out to be quite different from the original, to the disappointment of the pet owner who pays $50,000. In the case of CC, the donor cat, Rainbow, was shy, while CC was curious and playful, and the two cats looked very different. This happened because the interactions between the environment and the genes change how an organism will ultimately turn out. The environment influences how a cell or an organism uses its genes and so influences the outcome. Two organisms with the same genetic material grown in different environments can turn out to be very different from one another.

Stop and Consider

Some states are debating whether or not to permit the cloning of pets. What do you think? Should the cloning of pets be permitted or banned?

Another use for cloned animals is to create many copies of genetically altered mice or other research animals that mimic human diseases. These **transgenic animals** have their genes altered or new genes inserted that cause them to have the same symptoms as a human with a particular disease. An example of this is seen in mice that have had human immune system genes inserted in their genome so that they express the same proteins as human T cells. These transgenic mice can be infected with the human immunodeficiency virus (HIV), enabling scientists to test cures on animals before testing them on humans. These transgenic animals are very difficult to create in a laboratory and it is frequently impossible to recreate an animal that proves to be a useful research model for a particular disease. Through cloning, many genetically identical animals can be created to eliminate this problem. This is a very powerful research tool because it eliminates much of the variability that makes experiments on animals hard to interpret.

There is also the possibility of saving endangered animal species by cloning more genetic copies of these animals. Someday it may even be possible to bring back recently extinct animals through cloning. To accomplish this kind of cloning, scientists would have to isolate genomic DNA from preserved tissue samples and use this DNA to create a cloned version of the extinct animal. However, because DNA degrades as it ages, bringing back long extinct animals will most likely never be possible.

Finally, cloning animals is the only way to learn enough about the cloning process so that it may one day be safely and ethically used for human cloning. While it has not been determined whether cloning humans will ever be attempted, it remains a likely possibility. In the next chapter, we will learn that even if human cloning is made illegal around the world, it is likely that someone somewhere will have the desire, the funds, and the knowledge to pursue it, even if it is unwise.

ETHICAL QUESTIONS ABOUT ANIMAL RESEARCH

Since the beginning of agriculture, humans have tried to breed animals to have the best and most useful traits. Through programs of **selective breeding** and **animal husbandry**, people have created new breeds of animals that can be used for our comfort and survival. Perhaps this long history of controlling animal reproduction is why the issue of animal cloning is not as complex an ethical question as human cloning. We are accustomed to doing what we want with animals for our own purposes. While human cloning has not yet been achieved, animals and other organisms are already commonly being cloned. The list of cloned organisms includes bacteria, plants, fruit flies, farm animals, research animals, and even pets. Nonetheless, there remain ethical considerations surrounding the practice of animal cloning. These include how to protect the welfare of the cloned animals, what are appropriate reasons to clone animals, and do the religions of the world have anything to tell us about the morality of cloning animals.

Ethical opinions about animal cloning are further influenced by the type of animal being cloned. Not surprisingly, there is much less objection to cloning less developed organisms, such as flies, than there is to cloning animals that people consider cute or keep as pets.

Often arguments against cloning animals are voiced by organizations and individuals concerned with animal welfare. These organizations include moderate groups like the American Society for the Prevention of Cruelty to Animals (ASPCA) as well as more radical groups like Animal Liberation Front (ALF) and People for the Ethical Treatment of Animals (PETA). The most passionate of these activists feel that any research using animals is cruel and immoral because of the harm and suffering inflicted on the research animals. Further, they believe that by engaging in this research, we are dehumanizing the human race. They view scientists who use animals for research as insensitive, arrogant, and cruel (Figure 3.6).

There is a long history in Western society of people who have felt that humans should not be given a privileged dominion over animals, even though many fundamental Western beliefs tell us that humans do have the right to use animals however they please. In the 17th century, during what was considered the Age of Enlightenment, philosophers such as René Descartes wrote that animals

Figure 3.6 Some people feel that animal cloning and research is unethical. The woman in this picture is protesting the use of animals in research.

were mechanistic. He viewed them more like machines that could be exploited to fulfill peoples' needs, reflecting attitudes of his time. During this period and before, many people believed that animals felt no pain and had no consciousness. Biblical passages stating that mankind had mastery and dominion over animals were taken literally and, at times, acted on to extremes. It was widely believed that humans were made in God's image and possessed a soul; animals had no souls and were created solely to serve mankind. Few people up to this point in Western societies gave animal welfare much thought, unless the animals were their property or pets. These views helped form the basis of attitudes toward animals at the beginning of the Industrial Revolution. Lingering effects of these views can still be seen in some modern attitudes toward animals. There are still people who have little regard for nonhuman life, believing that animals are simply on Earth to be exploited for human purposes.

On the other hand, for religious or philosophical reasons, there are people who feel that all life is sacred and should be respected and protected. These beliefs began to be widely considered in Western societies in the early 19th century as the public became more aware and thoughtful about how animals were treated and exploited for labor, food, and research. Scientists of the time gained important knowledge from experimental procedures such as **vivisection**, where live animals were used in surgical experiments. But the practice deeply disturbed Victorian society's gentile sensibilities. Medical researchers were viewed as being ghoulish and cruel people who conducted unnecessary research on helpless animals. This perception, in part, contributed to a general mistrust of science, which persists into modern times.

Public attitudes about using animals for research have evolved since the 17th century, leading to the modern animal rights movement. This movement arose as a means for its members to campaign against inhumane treatment of animals in agriculture, entertainment, research, or any other activity. These organizations are a part of a worldwide movement that tends to be well-funded and sophisticated, and their efforts have had a lasting influence on how we treat animals today. These organizations represent a wide range of attitudes toward the question of animal rights. ALF and PETA have been known to resort to civil disobedience or violence to bring their message to the public. However, this violence has caused many supporters to seek other peaceful ways to express their opinions regarding animal rights. The core philosophy of these groups is that if humanity learns to treat animals with respect and kindness, then we humans will also learn to treat each other with respect and kindness. There are now religious leaders in the Christian, Jewish, and Muslim faiths who also find support for animal protection in their religious beliefs. This concept of the sacredness of animals is a movement away from the ancient and traditional Judeo-Christian view in which God gave man dominion over animals and the implied right to use them as he pleases.

Many non-Western societies around the world also have religious and philosophical objections to animal exploitation. The Jains in India believe that people should not harm any living creature for any reason. Buddhism is another Eastern religion that teaches the unity of all living beings. Buddhists believe that every living thing possesses the Buddha-nature and all have the potential to become enlightened and so should not be harmed as

PRO or CON?

Scientists have been conducting research on animals in various forms long before the advent of modern biotechnology. What are your feelings about animal research? Do you support it or are you against it? What are some of the pros and cons of using animals for research?

they pursue this enlightenment. According to Buddhist teachings, human beings do not have a privileged, special place above and beyond the rest of living creatures.

Gradually, over the past few centuries, society (including scientific researchers) has come to view dominion over animals as a benevolent responsibility for all animals' welfare. Accompanying this change in attitude is a growing understanding that animals are not mechanistic as Descartes thought, but instead have consciousness and experience pain. Thanks in part to efforts of animal rights groups and exposure to beliefs from cultures that have greater reverence for animals, society is becoming more convinced that people are obligated to protect the welfare of animals. In an effort to protect the welfare of animals and ensure that they are treated ethically, the U.S. government passed the Animal Welfare Act. Since its adoption in 1966, the Animal Welfare Act has evolved to keep pace with the public's changing attitudes toward the humane treatment of animals. Today, this act provides guidelines that must be followed in all research that involves the use of animals, including cloning experiments.

There are members of the scientific community who feel it is unethical to use animals for research. Some scientists claim that scientific research can use model systems, other than live animals, that may be more reliable. These alternatives include using simpler organisms like bacteria, cell culture, or computer simulation. However, some scientists have shown that research conducted on animals provides very different results from those observed when research is conducted on human subjects. For example, many drugs that are effective on humans, such as penicillin, are ineffective or toxic in animals. Had scientists relied solely on animal testing to determine penicillin's safety in the 1930s and 1940s, it may never have been developed into a drug for human use. Penicillin is **teratogenic** (causes limb deformities) in rats and is toxic to guinea pigs, cats, and hamsters. Penicillin does not work at all in rabbits with infections because it is excreted by their kidneys before it can work. But in 1939, even after animal experiments gave ambiguous results, Howard Florey, Ernst Chain, and Norman Heatley chose to give this experimental drug to patients who were near death due to serious infections. The gamble worked and the patients recovered. A new miracle drug was discovered that might have been overlooked if results of only animal research had been considered.

If animals are not reliable experimental models for studying human biology and medical conditions, then the results of research on animals may be misleading when applied to humans. In that case, much of the medical research on animals may be unnecessary and wasteful, leading to needless harm to animals. Further, according to this view, if scientists rely on results of animal cloning experiments to demonstrate that human cloning is feasible and safe, there may be grave and unforeseen problems. The question of whether or not it is an acceptable risk to attempt human cloning based on the outcome of animal experiments will be explored in the chapter on human cloning.

ETHICAL USES FOR CLONING ANIMALS

Today, the scientific research community is acutely aware that any research involving animal cloning must meet the highly restrictive standards of humane treatment of animals as specified in the Animal Welfare Act. Most of today's mainstream researchers believe that there is a great deal to be learned from studying animal cloning that can be learned in no other way. In certain situations, they even believe that the importance of what they can learn outweighs concerns for animal welfare. These scientists claim that knowledge gained from animal cloning research directly helps to find cures and treatments for human disease and suffering. It is also likely that the knowledge gained will contribute to improving the quality of animal life as well. This reasoning is why many mainstream scientists hold strong convictions that much good can come from animal research and animal cloning.

There are times when animal cloning is acceptable and times when animal cloning is unacceptable. Cloning is a risky and expensive process with mixed outcomes for the animals involved. Is it appropriate to spend $50,000 to clone a single cat? Some critics claim that all the resources used to clone CC and Little Nicky could have been used to improve the lives of hundreds of homeless cats. As we have discussed, there is no guarantee that a clone will be exactly like, or even closely resemble, its donor. But this is what pet owners expect when they pay $50,000.

Another consideration is that animal cloning could be used to save or bring back endangered or extinct animals. On the surface, that would appear to be a great gift to the world, but if cloning brings back extinct animals, where will they live? Maintaining a collection of extinct animals in captivity does not ensure their survival nor provide them with a quality life. The movie *Jurassic Park* and its sequels made this point over and over again. Further, keeping small populations of an animal species alive only in zoos has proven difficult and expensive. It can lead to problems with interbreeding that weaken the animals.

One reason that animal species become extinct is because their natural habitat is lost. This can be due to either the land becoming so polluted that the animals cannot tolerate the conditions or because land is altered by human development and use. Without a natural habitat very similar to the habitat where an animal species originally evolved, it has proven virtually impossible to reestablish wild populations. Millions of dollars have been spent in this effort with limited success because animal species evolve to fit into a particular natural niche where they survive the best. If that niche no longer exists, then that animal species may no longer have a place in nature to fit in. A better approach to preserving and protecting endangered species may be to determine why the organism has become endangered and then take steps to correct the problem. This would make the chances of success more likely. Then perhaps replacement clones would have a chance to reestablish their species in their natural habitats.

As discussed, animal cloning can be used to increase the number of animals with desirable traits. By combining cloning with genetic engineering, in which particular traits are inserted into an animal's genome, large numbers of genetically engineered animals can be created. While this could be a very powerful and beneficial use of cloning technology, there are concerns. If genes are inserted into animals used as food, will that alter the food, creating possible health risks? (This question will be further explored in Chapter 6.) While no health issues have been suggested with these foods so far, there remains a potential risk. If a gene is used to engineer an animal's genome and it somehow imparts a toxic property to the animal, then it could be harmful to the animal's welfare or perhaps to someone who consumes it. There is fear that some of these genes could be passed from the cloned animal to wild animals in nature, thereby altering the wild stock. In Maine, there are fears that this could happen to genetically engineered fish that might be farmed in open waters.

Ethical questions related to this issue include which genes are selected for the engineering process, how much the public should be told about these transgenic animals if they become part of the food supply, and whether this process might cause harmful effects and unnecessary suffering in the animals. There are numerous cases where commercial interests have overlooked risk to the public or to other living organisms in the interest of maximizing profits. This has lead to widespread public concern in Maine where these fish are being farmed. Some people are very distrustful of this technology. There are local governments trying hard to block attempts by fish growers to obtain permits. Who should determine how much risk is acceptable to the residents of Maine and their waters?

CONNECTIONS

Animals have played a very important role in human history. Without animals, humans would never have been able to create the advanced civilization we live in today. Further, we will continue to require the help of animals as we advance to even greater human achievements. It is up to us to find ways to express our gratitude. The Chinese hold festivals to honor their animals. Perhaps we should find ways to do the same. In any case, it is an indication of moral strength to remember the debt we owe to animals and to treat them well as we continue to use them for our purposes.

FOR MORE INFORMATION

For more information about the concepts discussed in this chapter, search the Web using the following keywords:

Nature vs. nurture, Roslin Institute, Dolly the sheep, Somatic cell nuclear transfer (SCNT), Hemophilia, Factor IX, Polly the sheep, Genetic Savings and Clone, PETA, ASPCA

4

Human Cloning: Should Humans Be Cloned?

As of 2005, no one has convincingly demonstrated that human cloning has been accomplished or even attempted, beyond creating an embryo with only a few cells. However, Clonaid, a company created solely to develop human cloning, claims to have cloned as many as 13 people as of 2004. These claims are unsubstantiated, but Clonaid has sought out independent scientists to examine and compare the DNA from the alleged cloned babies to that of the adult donors.

Human clones, which are referred to as identical twins, occur in nature and are actually a common phenomenon, occurring once in 250 human births. Identical twins are born with exactly the same DNA, in fact with DNA that is likely to be more similar than that of most clones and their donors. Only a female cloning herself by donating her own fertile egg and using her own somatic cell DNA would have the exact same DNA as her clone and be as genetically similar as identical twins. This is because if the egg used for cloning is provided by an unrelated donor, it will contain mitochondrial DNA that is different from the donor's mitochondrial DNA. Only if the egg donor is a member of the maternal line, such as the female herself or her mother or her maternal grandmother, would the mitochondrial DNA also be the same in this clone. This is because mitochondrial DNA is always passed down from the mother to her offspring, never from the father to his offspring.

We already know a considerable amount about the likely outcomes of human cloning because of society's ongoing fascination with twins (Figure 4.1). Twin studies have proven a very powerful method of comparing the degree to which genes or environment influence growth and development. These studies address the same Nature vs. Nurture question discussed earlier. But the question posed in the title of this chapter asks whether or not we should clone humans artificially. Is it morally acceptable to make an identical twin of someone who is already alive? Is this somehow physically or ethically different from naturally occurring twins?

It should be emphasized that arguments for and against cloning are speculative. Since the technology to clone humans has not yet been developed and used, as far as we know, there is no way to know with certainty how human cloning will affect us as a species. The technology may lead to a better future with many new medical options or to a nightmarish future with unimagined horrors. On the other hand, the technology may prove to have little noticeable impact at all. However, serious and careful consideration of human cloning by society is very important, especially for the younger generations that will have to live in this future world.

METHODS FOR CLONING HUMANS

How would humans be cloned if someone chose to try it now? Two possible approaches are available and already used for animal

Figure 4.1 Shown here is a group of twins at the Twins Day Festival in Twinsburg, Ohio, where each year thousands of twins gather to celebrate. Scientists from all over the country visit the festival looking for twins willing to participate in twin studies.

cloning, as mentioned in the last chapter. These include twinning, which is not considered true cloning, and somatic cell nuclear transfer (SCNT), which is what is usually meant when the term *cloning* is used. Neither method has been proven to be completely reliable in animal testing. Other methods are likely to be developed in the future and these could prove safer and more reliable than current methods. If this happens, then some of the reservations concerning human cloning might disappear.

Twinning has been suggested as a means to improve the efficiency of *in vitro* **fertilization** (IVF). Current IVF procedures create one fertilized **embryo** from one egg and one **sperm**. While it is easy to get huge numbers of donated sperm, it is difficult to harvest female eggs. The procedure is physically demanding on the woman who is the egg donor and is often performed several times before a successful pregnancy is achieved. Since IVF is also expensive, it would make sense to develop means to maximize the number of implantable embryos from each fertilized egg. This would be less costly as well as less demanding on the female egg donor. Twinning embryos created by IVF would make larger numbers of implantable embryos available (Figure 4.2).

Twinning could be used to separate the first few cells in IVF-created embryos. Each of these separated embryo cells would have the potential to develop into a new complete embryo. In this way, a single fertilization event could create all the embryos required to achieve a successful IVF pregnancy. If more than one embryo was implanted, as is usual with IVF procedures, the result would be the birth of identical twins that would also be clones from the same fertilized egg. The only difference between these clones and natural twins would be the way they were created. If twinning of humans were determined to be safe, there would probably be less controversy about it than there is about SCNT cloning. IVF is now widely used by infertile couples and the majority of people around the world consider it an acceptable practice. It is considered different from SCNT cloning because IVF relies on a male's sperm joining with a female's **oocyte**, which is the normal way humans are conceived, even if it is occurs outside the human body. Still, some groups object to this way of creating a child. Most of these objections are based on religious beliefs rather than on concerns for the safety of the technology.

SCNT cloning as practiced in animal cloning was described in the last chapter. If it were used for human cloning, it would be technically very similar. The nucleus of a human egg cell would be removed by microinjection. A donor's **somatic cell** would be the

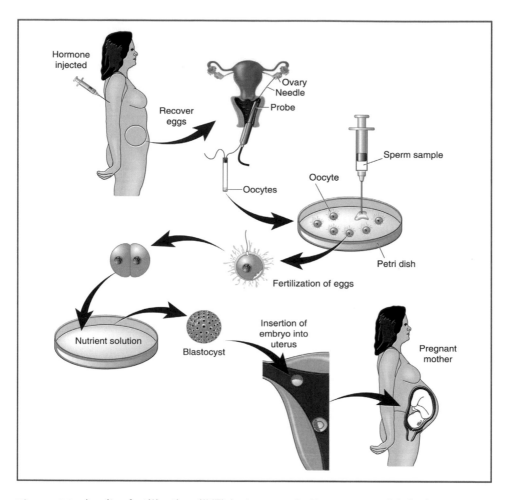

Figure 4.2 *In vitro* fertilization (IVF) in humans is the process of bringing an egg and sperm together artificially in a laboratory to create an embryo. The woman is first treated with high levels of hormones to encourage superovulation (release of multiple eggs). Next, a physician has to manually harvest eggs by laparoscopy through an incision in the abdomen or by using a needle and ultrasound that is inserted through the vagina. The harvested eggs, or ova, are then placed in a petri dish and mixed with sperm from the male. The sperm and eggs unite in the petri dish and each fertilized egg begins to divide to become an embryo. If the embryo is determined to be healthy, it is then implanted into a woman who will be the birth mother.

source of the DNA. This DNA would be injected into the enucleated egg cell and the egg would be stimulated to start dividing, either chemically or by an electrical current. Once the fertilized human embryo reached the proper stage, it would be inserted into a woman's womb, where it would develop into a fetus and then a child.

REPRODUCTIVE VERSUS THERAPEUTIC CLONING OF HUMANS

There are basically two motivations for performing human cloning: to produce children (**reproductive cloning**) and for medical research (**therapeutic cloning**). In therapeutic cloning, the cells are not permitted to develop past the first few cycles of division before growth is arrested. In other words, these embryos are never implanted into a womb and never progress to the fetal stage. This distinction is important because there are different ethical considerations for each type of cloning. Some people object to reproductive cloning, but feel that therapeutic cloning is justifiable.

Reproductive cloning might be used for several reasons. Without considering the morality of each use, here is a sample of those reasons:

- Parents might want to replace a child they had lost.

- A clone might be needed as an organ donor for another family member.

- Infertile couples might choose cloning so that at least one parent would be genetically related to the child.

- If one parent had a harmful genetic trait that he or she did not want passed on to the next generation, cloning could provide a genetically related offspring without that trait. Parents might want to select certain traits, such as increased intelligence or increased athletic ability, which could be engineered into an embryo during the cloning process.

- A person with traits thought to be potentially valuable to society could be cloned. A clone as intelligent as Albert Einstein or as talented as Audrey Hepburn might be created.

- Genetic cloning might be seen as a way to achieve genetic immortality; a person could be cloned, and then have the resulting clone recloned, continuing this generation after generation.

Therapeutic cloning also has many possible applications. Scientists believe that invaluable knowledge about human development could be gained from cloned embryos. Much has already been learned from studying unwanted human embryos that are left over once IVF procedures have successfully produced the desired number of childbirths that a couple wants. Using cloned embryos would give scientists more control over experimental design leading to more effective experimentation. This research might one day help scientists discover new therapies to cure genetic diseases such as how to insert or repair a specific gene in an embryo. Cloned embryos are predicted to be a valuable source of embryonic stem cells, which may prove to be powerful therapeutic tools for degenerative diseases and organ and tissue replacement. Therapeutic cloning would also permit scientists to learn more about the critical early stages of human development; this would greatly advance our ability to cure many developmental disorders and diseases.

WHY IS HUMAN CLONING CONTROVERSIAL?

Since it is a virtual certainty that no humans have ever been cloned, much is unknown about the effects human cloning would have on the clone or how human cloning might change our society and culture. Whatever effects cloning might have, cloning would be like opening Pandora's Box, because there would be no way to turn back once the technology was developed and in use. In response to the general concern of the public, governments, the bioscience community, religious communities, ethicists, and many other public and private organizations, there is an ongoing debate surrounding human cloning. This debate is viewed as critically important. Even if no consensus results, the debate will help us prepare for the effects of human cloning should it ever come to pass.

It is a credit to humanity that the debate is happening now, before human cloning has been accomplished, so we can ensure that no harm will come from this powerful technology. In the past, humanity has generally played catch-up whenever a new technology has negative consequences. There is a confused scramble to figure out how to contain the damage and develop acceptable policies to address the problems. For example, consider the effects of global warming we are experiencing now and how slow the people and governments of the world are at agreeing on what must be done to stop the warming. People do not want global warming to harm the planet, but they also want to have big cars and to be conspicuous consumers of every new technology. Meanwhile, large chunks of ice are breaking off the polar ice shelf and melting, birds are stopping their migration, and weather patterns are changing. So, it is a hopeful sign for humanity that we are confronting the issue of human cloning before it creates problems for humanity, even if the outcome of the discussion may not be to one's liking.

Some critics feel that human cloning is one of the greatest ethical questions of our time because human cloning may fundamentally affect what it means to be human. These critics have expressed grave concerns that by giving people the choice of duplicating themselves or someone else, humans would become a type of commodity. We would change the meaning of the act of human procreation from a random mixing of parental genes, occurring through sexual reproduction, to a type of planned manufacturing of humans in which the clones' genes are predetermined and based on consumer choice. The outcome of natural birth is a unique combination of the genes of two parents that results in a unique individual created through the act of conception. For humans, there is less than a 1 in 8,388,608 chance that any two parents will give the same exact combination of genes to two offspring. The only exception is the case of identical twins. Some people believe that the act of human conception is influenced by a divine force or is, in itself, a divine act. The unpredictability of natural human conception ensures each individual's uniqueness, making each person separate and distinct. What would happen to the human race if this were not so? Would the concepts of self and identity be forever changed?

On the other hand, supporters of human cloning feel that humanity would derive great benefit from this technology. Most of these supporters believe that human cloning should only be used for research and therapeutic purposes, rather than reproductive purposes. At the earliest stages of embryological development, a clone could provide answers to important questions about human biology or provide potentially invaluable stem cells for regenerative medical procedures. However, a minority among the supporters of human cloning believe that human cloning to produce children should also be permitted. Since twins are the result of natural births and these twins suffer no apparent harmful consequences from sharing the same genetic material with one another, why should a cloned person have trouble sharing the same genes with the donor? This highly debated view will be covered in later sections of the book.

Arguments against cloning

Most people seem to agree that reproductive cloning should not be pursued now, given the unreliability of the technology that would be used to create clones. Many even feel that reproductive cloning, regardless of its reliability, should never be pursued and perhaps should be banned by law. But a legal ban against human cloning for reproductive purposes may not be fully effective in preventing attempts to clone humans. Many groups and individuals proclaim that they will pursue human cloning at all costs. Even so, a ban would greatly reduce the likelihood that the technology would be used because fear of the consequences of ignoring the ban would be a deterrent in most cases. Why is agreement so widespread that reproductive cloning should not be attempted?

The most universal concern about cloning for human repro-duction comes from our inability to test the safety of cloning humans. The only way to be certain that human cloning is safe would be to try to do it. Current attempts to clone animals have shown that there is tremendous uncertainty in the outcomes. To most people, this indicates that cloning is too unpredictable and not yet understood well enough to be tried on humans. Even those who believe that human cloning will someday be safe find it far too risky to be used now. For example, the success rate in animal cloning experiments has been very low, as discussed previously, with 277 tries to get one healthy live birth in the case of Dolly the sheep. Even today, the success rate for cloning mammals typically remains low. In addition, though Dolly at first seemed normal and robust to her handlers, she had to be **euthanized** at age six when she developed an unusual arthritic condition. This is only half the normal life span for sheep. Did this condition occur because Dolly was cloned, or was it just a naturally occurring health problem? Scientists do not know the answer. For many people, this level of uncertainty makes human cloning for reproductive purposes unthinkable at this point. Most people are unwilling to use technology that has the potential to produce abnormal children. Imagine the horror and outrage the world would express if human cloning produced terribly deformed or subnormal clones.

Another concern is that if humans are cloned, family relation-ship issues could arise from the confused boundaries between generations. We can distinguish three categories of parents based on the role that each parent plays in a child's life. These include three kinds of mothers and two kinds of fathers. There are the genetic mother and father, or in the case of a clone, the one parent who provides DNA for the child. There is a birth mother or gestational mother, who may or may not be the same as the genetic mother. This mother gestates the child in her womb and gives birth to the child. There are also the social mother and father who raise the

Eugenics

Eugenics is the study and use of selective breeding to improve humans or animals. The idea was first proposed in 1883 by Sir Francis Galton. It may be surprising to learn that during the early 20th century, eugenics was very popular in the United States. Medical practice and some laws were based on the idea that the human race could be improved by encouraging certain people to procreate and discouraging others from procreating. The belief in eugenics as a means of improving Americans was so popular that school textbooks taught the concepts. Certain American families were selected as examples of positive eugenics. These families were even honored at public events.

After World War II, the Nazis on trial claimed that they used American ideas of eugenics as their inspiration for their version of eugenics. As a result, the practice of and belief in eugenics has fallen into disfavor worldwide. Since the end of World War II, those who advocate for the use of eugenics even to attempt to limit the spread of genetic disease or who propose to use eugenic methods to improve a human trait are strongly criticized.

Today, with our greater understanding of genetics and the vast knowledge we have learned from research like the Human Genome Project, there are again discussions about how humans can use genetic knowledge to improve our health. Thanks to the lessons learned from the Nazis, there is great caution in adapting any methods or technologies that would introduce selective breeding for humans. However, it is important not to dismiss a medical advance that could help suffering people only on the grounds that it could be considered a form of eugenics. It is important to weigh the motivation behind the use of genetic technology and respect people's right to make their own reproductive choices. This is where earlier believers in eugenics stepped over the line in taking away peoples' freedom of choice.

child. When cloned children are added to this mix of parental types, some very complex family relationships can arise.

If a woman chooses to become the genetic mother to a cloned child, and another woman is selected to be the birth mother, what will be the relationship between the social father (the husband of the genetic mother) and the cloned child? In this case, the genetic mother is now a genetic twin of her child clone. They are actually genetic siblings. In some cases, the genetic mother could even be the birth mother. If so, the genetic mother would give birth to her own identical twin and the clone is the sister-in-law of the social father as well as his adopted daughter. Then one must consider the woman who donated the egg; could she develop feelings of family relationship toward the clone? Some aspects described so far may not seem very different from a typical adoption situation, or a surrogate pregnancy as practiced today in IVF births. It may even resemble the genetic relationships in a stepfamily, but relationships could be even more confusing. The cloned child, a girl, would look exactly like the genetic mother, who is the wife of the social father. What if the social parents divorce? Perhaps the social father, who has no genetic relationship to the cloned child, would be reminded of his wife when she was young. Might the social father become confused in his feeling toward the cloned girl and try to relive his youth? Now, consider that since the cloned girl is essentially a twin to the genetic mother, she is also a genetic daughter to her maternal grandparents. As a genetic daughter, does she have rights of inheritance? Do the mother's parents, who are the actual genetic mother and father of the clone, have parental rights? Unique family situations that would arise as a result of cloning might produce special difficulties that our society is not accustomed to confronting.

There are other compelling reasons why reproductive cloning presents ethical concerns. In a culture where we have easy access to birth control, many children are planned for by their parents. But a cloned child's birth is not only planned for, that child's entire genetic makeup is planned. Through cloning, a child's parents may develop unreasonable expectations for the child, because the child's genetic makeup and identity have been "specified" or "made to order" through the process of selecting the donor DNA. Parents with this type of control over the genetic makeup of their children may find that they have stronger expectations for a certain outcome. If the desired outcome is not realized, could this lead to disappointment that harms natural family ties?

Another consideration is that, in some ways, the cloned child's genetic life has already been lived by the DNA donor. Might this affect the child's view of him or herself? Would a cloned child who exactly resembles one parent experience identity or individuality issues? Would there be unjust expectations that the cloned child go through life in the same way as the "original"? If a deadly genetic disorder should appear in the DNA donor, would this create unhealthy anticipation in the clone because of the certainty that he or she would also die from the same genetic disorder? If the DNA donor was an outstanding athlete, would parental ambition force the clone to pursue sports to fulfill their genetic potential just as the donor did? Perhaps in this situation a parent may expect to become wealthy from the clone's success. Is this an acceptable use of cloning for procreation?

Developing a technology in which parents can control the genetics of their children may lead to the production of designer babies. This would combine cloning with genetic engineering. Parents could pick and choose which genetic traits they wanted their baby to have. These babies would be "produced" to parents' specifications rather than conceived through the naturally occurring uncertainty of sexual reproduction. Children born today are in most ways "surprises" to their parents. Even though now, by using ultrasound, it is possible to know the sex of a baby, parents still have to wait and watch their child grow and develop to see the type of person he or she will become. If parents develop expectations that they can demand certain genetic traits in a child, does the situation begin to resemble consumerism? Becoming a parent may take on aspects of shopping for the genes we desire to see in our children. Parents may want only the best genetically cloned children with the best genes. Will fashion trends in baby traits develop? Perhaps parents will prefer certain fashionable eye colors, hair colors, and perhaps even complexions.

If this sounds unlikely, consider the social engineering now occurring in China and India, where technology allows the determination of the sex of the fetus early in pregnancy and the abortion of females. In these cultures, boys are more desirable than girls for ancient cultural reasons. After years of people choosing to have boys rather than girls, there is now a shortage of women of child-bearing age. In some situations, a single female must be wife to several males. People in these countries know that this is a big social problem, but they continue the practice of selecting boys over girls.

How will the human race be altered if cloning and genetic engineering technologies become available? If the technology is very expensive, then only the very rich will be able to have the best quality clones as children. Will poor people have to settle for "the luck of the draw" through natural birth? Could this lead to greater differences between the very wealthy "enhanced" people and the poorer "natural" population?

If cloning humans ever does lead to the creation of "enhanced" children, then the ability to select genetic traits for our offspring raises the possibility of a new form of eugenics. In a society that accepts eugenics, it might be acceptable to classify humans on a genetic basis, as happens in Andrew Niccol's 1997 movie *GATTACA*, which portrays a world in which there is a genetic **caste** system with two classes: the superior genetically "enhanced" upper-class, who are born or "created" using genetic engineering and other enhancement technologies, and the inferior underclass, which includes people born naturally, just as we are today. The movie explores the psychological and social effects of this class structure. Even though the main character, played by Ethan Hawke, possesses natural abilities to excel, he is not permitted to use them to pursue the career he has always dreamed of because he has only natural genes and was not genetically enhanced before birth. He can only achieve his goal and overcome the effects of eugenics by concealing his true origins and pretending to be genetically "enhanced."

Another fear about this new eugenics is that we might one day breed a race of clones designed genetically to be placid slaves. In this very frightening scenario, eugenics is envisioned as a tool to suppress people. Aldous Huxley's book *Brave New World*, written

When Does Science Fiction Become Reality?

In *GATTACA*, the 1997 film by Andrew Niccol, the idea of genetic perfection has led to a society where there are two classes of people. The genetically enhanced are the ruling class while those born as we are today are considered the inferior "in-valids." Highly advanced DNA analysis technology permits instantaneous detection of who is who as well as one's biological future based on the quality of one's genes. Ethan Hawke plays the character of Vincent, an in-valid, who was born to careless parents. Vincent's younger brother, Anton, however, was engineered with genetic enhancements. The two brothers have an ongoing competition that constantly reminds Vincent of his status as an in-valid. However, after years of working in menial jobs, Vincent decides to pursue his dreams that have been denied to him because of his inferior genes. By using false genetic samples collected from Jerome, an enhanced athlete whose injuries have left him a paraplegic, Vincent is able to gain a job at GATTACA in the space program. While working there, he also wins the heart of Irene, an enhanced beauty played by Uma Thurman. All is going well until a murder is committed at GATTACA and a single eyelash from Vincent is found at the scene of the crime. The DNA in the eyelash is determined to be from an in-valid whose DNA is not on record as an employee at GATTACA. It seems that it is only a matter of time before Anton, one of the police investigators, discovers that the eyelash belongs to his brother Vincent.

GATTACA addresses numerous fears that we have about how genetic technology might be misused in the future. There are many imagined ways that this powerful in 1931, further explores a society in which people are cloned to fit into specified genetically engineered classes (Figure 4.3). Huxley's book describes a world that appears utopian on the surface. However, upon closer scrutiny, we find that freedom of choice has been stripped away and replaced by a false, drug-induced complacency. This theme is also seen in the *Matrix* film trilogy, which shows a future world based on computer technology in which machines use cloned people to produce energy to run their machine world. These clones are kept in special pods, but a virtual reality system, known as the Matrix, fools the humans into thinking they are living a normal life.

technology could be misused to suppress our freedom and alter our world in ways we would not like. If we will someday be able to genetically enhance our children, it is likely that not everyone will be able to afford the procedure. Those who cannot afford it may rightly wonder if their "naturally" born children will be able to compete with "enhanced" children. If not, they could, as in the movie, become part of an "underclass." How will parents feel about condemning a child to this life just because of how the child was conceived?

Genetic privacy is another issue raised in *GATTACA*. It is likely that it will become easier and easier to analyze DNA as depicted in the movie. Someday a person's genes may be used to make decisions that affect how that person is viewed by business or the government. Perhaps insurance companies will want to use this information to determine who to insure and who not to insure. Current laws exist in some states banning this type of genetic discrimination. In the United States, the "Justice for All Act" had allowed the Combined DNA Index System (CODIS) to be expanded. Now not only can the DNA profile of those convicted of violent crimes be included, but in some states the DNA profile of those simply charged with certain crimes can be included, even those later found innocent. The American Civil Liberties Union has expressed concern that this information could someday be made available to employers or be used to influence decisions unrelated to crime and law enforcement. The world we see in *GATTACA* may not be so farfetched or faraway.

Figure 4.3 In his futuristic novel <u>Brave new World</u>, Aldous Huxley (seen here) has wrote about a world free of war and suffering that exists 600 years in the future. People live only to enjoy leisure and pleasure, but at what cost? There are no personal freedoms except for those allowed by the 10 "controllers" that rule the world. People are created by cloning and are kept complacent by using a drug called "soma." There are five separate classes of cloned people that do not interact with one another. Is this utopia or a society of slaves?

An equally scary possibility for cloning is that a person might be cloned without knowing it. It only takes a single adult cell to supply the genetic material needed to start a clone. Would it be acceptable for people to "steal" cells from a famous person, say George Clooney or Julia Roberts, and use the stolen DNA to produce and sell clones to interested "collector parents"? It would only take a few live cells from hair roots, a blood sample, or cheek scraping, which would not be hard to obtain.

Arguments for cloning

Understandably, there are more arguments against human cloning than in favor of it because fear of the unknown is a powerful force. Frightening stories about cloning capture our imaginations by filling us with dread. On the other hand, stories of cures for the afflicted and hope for the infertile tend to hold our attention only if the issue directly impacts us or someone we know. In other words, unless you are sick with pancreatic cancer, you do not tend to read about all the possible cures for pancreatic cancer. But people seem to enjoy scaring themselves by imagining how horrible it could be to have clones in our midst.

Frequently, when a new technology is introduced with the potential to change our lives, the public reacts with concern or outrage. However, over time, many of these "scary" new technologies have proven to be good and useful. Even if everyone does not see them as good or useful, those technologies often become a generally accepted part of life upon which people come to depend. For example, when the birth control pill was first introduced in the early 1960s, many embraced the new freedom from the risk of pregnancy. However, some religious groups strongly objected and forbid their members to use this method of birth control, which was viewed as a sinful technology. Today, some groups still feel this way, and voice this view as part of their human right of free expression. However, for those who have chosen to use this form of contraception, it has significantly altered lifestyle choices. Sex is less closely tied to pro-creation. People can practice family planning with greater control over desired family size. Nowadays, this technology is an integral part of our society and is widely viewed as good.

> ### Stop and Consider
>
> **Think about some of the issues associated with human cloning. What are your feelings on human cloning? Are you for or against it? Do you feel that, if it should happen, there should be certain restrictions? Why or why not?**

This is not to say that any new technology will eventually be accepted by society and viewed as good by most people. It is very challenging to predict how a specific technology will impact society. Will it produce more good than harm or vice versa? This is true of cloning as well. Cloning is by no means the first technology that has been widely debated. It is, however, among the first to be so controversial before it is even possible to achieve.

There are many arguments in support of human cloning. Some are fairly easy to accept, such as elimination of genetic disease. Others may seem wrong to us as we read about them now, but how are we to predict how future societies will come to view these uses for cloning? After all, many people vehemently protested the "horseless carriages" (automobiles) at the beginning of the 20th century, claiming they were noisy, dirty, and against the natural order; the automobile was even called a "Devil Wagon." Now how are cars viewed by society?

The following is a sampling of positive uses for cloning as well as comments, justifications, and concerns.

- We can ask who has the right to restrict people from choosing to perform human cloning. If a person chooses to have a child by cloning because this is the best option for him or her, should the government be able to restrict this person's wish to procreate? There have been other attempts by governments, including that of the United States, to control human reproduction, all of which have eventually been judged unacceptable in a free democratic society. At one time, criminals and people with mental handicaps were forcibly sterilized to prevent them from having children because it was believed that this would eventually decrease the number of people carrying genes that cause criminal behavior or mental retardation. This is one of the darkest examples of how eugenics was used in the United States. By 1941, there were eugenic laws in 30 American states that mandated this type of control over an individual's right to reproduce. All of these laws have been repealed because it is unconstitutional in our society to limit a person's reproductive rights.

- Cloning may offer the potential of improving the quality of many human lives by developing new cures and therapies. Cloning may make it possible to repair or insert genes that would cure a genetic defect. This would be a type of therapeutic cloning. There was enough support for this type of cloning by members of the President's Council on Bioethics that one of the council's final recommendations gave qualified support for therapeutic cloning.

- Cloning may be useful in enhancing the genetic makeup of the clone. While today most people seem to think this is a bad idea, some day society may judge some enhanced traits as acceptable. For example, suppose that a trait could be added to a child's genome that would ensure that the child would never develop cancer. Even if today's parents are morally opposed to this use of cloning, it is easy to believe that over time, if the procedure proves safe, increasing numbers of parents would opt for this enhancement to protect their child from a horrible disease or for other equally enticing enhancements that could come along.

• Parents who have lost a child or someone who has lost a loved one may choose to clone a replacement to keep his or her memory alive. Even now, as discussed in the previous chapter, people are starting to replace lost pets with cloned copies. These people are told that the clone is not an exact replica of the lost pet, but still feel they will be comforted by knowing that at least some aspect of their original pet is still with them. Some grieving parents might seek a means to clone lost children.

• There may be a value to society for cloning people who demonstrate great talents or intellects. Imagine a world where your favorite celebrities or the best thinkers can be recycled and kept forever to benefit humanity. However, we must remember that cloning does not result in the same person being born. The clones from these special individuals would have the same genetic potential as the original. However, this motivation for cloning may seem morally wrong to some people.

• Nontraditional couples, such as same sex couples, could use cloning to have biologically related children.

Not all aspiring parents feel it is necessary to be genetically related to their children, but some do. These people want a level of biological connection through sharing an inherited genome.

- Cloning could be useful for screening embryos for genetic diseases to prevent children from being born with these diseases. Now it is possible to test a fetus for genetic disorders to give the parents the option to terminate a pregnancy if a genetic disorder is detected. This is a very wrenching decision for parents, made worse because screening results are often unavailable until the second trimester of pregnancy. The use of cloning technology in conjunction with IVF procedures is another way to screen the embryo before it is implanted into the mother's uterus for a procedure such as IVF. This would help eliminate the need for second trimester abortions.

In the book *Remaking Eden,* Lee Silver addresses many of the concerns voiced by opponents of human cloning. He presents an informed view that is not biased by anti-science fears. In his discussion, he makes the premise for argument's sake that human cloning will be shown to be a safe procedure, since safety is the most universal objection to human cloning.

Silver points out that laws created to ban human cloning can never be effective in the long run, because the decision to clone will be made by people exercising their freedom to reproduce as they wish. We live in a "marketplace society," so if there is a demand for cloning to produce children, then someone will offer it, even if it has to be done in a remote location where the laws do not apply. Since a clone will look just like anyone born naturally, there will be no effective way to detect who is and who is not cloned without using genetic testing, which requires consent. Human cloning may someday be commercialized; already groups have Websites accepting names of people interested in paying for services to create cloned babies. These sites offer information to parents so they can learn more about having cloned babies.

WHO IS CLONING HUMANS AND WHY?

As mentioned, a number of groups and individuals claim that they are working to clone humans for research, for commercial reasons, or for religious reasons. Some of these efforts are being made by scientists considered part of the legitimate research community, while others are made by people who are viewed with skepticism, such as the Raelians, a cult-like religious group who established the company known as Clonaid. Why do these groups want to make human clones, and are their motives acceptable?

In 2001, Advanced Cell Technology (ACT) in Worcester, Massachusetts, announced the creation of the first cloned human embryo using SCNT. The only purpose of creating these embryos was to harvest stem cells, not to create humans through cloning. Stem cells may prove to be powerful therapeutic agents to cure degenerative diseases. If this proves true, many people would be helped, and there is a huge market for such technology. The embryos did not survive past the six-cell stage and so scientists were unable to isolate the stem cells they sought to create. Even so, public reaction to the announcement was significant, rekindling the debate for and against human cloning.

In 2004, South Korean scientists successfully cloned human embryos for the same purpose as ACT, using similar techniques. In this case, they successfully isolated stem cells that could be used for further research. South Korea has since banned cloning for human reproduction, but will continue to permit therapeutic cloning. Some countries, including Great Britain, permit limited human cloning for therapeutic research only, while other countries such as Germany have total bans.

As mentioned above, Clonaid announced the birth of the first human clone in 2002, but their claims have not been substantiated by anyone outside of their company. They claim to have performed the successful cloning of at least 13 more children since 2002. The identity of these children has been kept a secret. Clonaid and the Raelians report that their intention is to clone humans so that they can make human beings immortal. To do this, they are first learning how to clone humans. The next step, they say, will be to discover a way to transfer a person's memories into the clone and thereby become immortal. Of course, this is viewed as an outlandish goal by the mainstream research community.

Two other scientists have been noted in the news for their claims that they were working to produce cloned humans. Both Dr. Severino Antinori of Italy, known for helping a 62-year-old woman have a child, and Dr. Panos Zavos from Kentucky claim to have been involved in attempts to clone humans for reproduction. Dr. Antinori has claimed that the cloning has succeeded, though he produced no evidence to back this up. Dr. Zavos has said that his attempts were unsuccessful and has gone on to develop his technique further. The motivation driving these scientists appears to be their search for fame and profit. Dr. Zavos has been quoted as saying that there would be a "great deal" of money in offering cloning technology to couples having fertility problems. While this justification for pursuing cloning technology may sound self-serving, does this motivation differ from that of other entrepreneurs? People have always sought ways to find fame and fortune. Throughout history, these efforts have often also harmed society, yet in the United States we believe in the freedom of a capitalist economy, meaning that people have the right to pursue whatever business they choose as long as they are not breaking the law. Cloning has not been made illegal in the United States as of 2005.

GOVERNMENT ACTIONS TOWARD HUMAN CLONING

Many governments around the world, as well as the United Nations, have taken up the debate about human cloning. These debates generally lead either to a total ban on any type of human cloning or a ban on reproductive cloning that permits therapeutic cloning. Some governments, including the United States, are still debating the issue and have not yet established a policy toward human cloning. The fact that this debate is being taken seriously is generally considered a healthy sign that we will avoid rash decisions to either ban or permit human cloning before all scientific and ethical considerations are examined.

In the United States, therapeutic cloning of human embryos was the only type of cloning that the President's Council on Bioethics endorsed in its report to the President in 2002. Even so, only a minority of the council held this view. The council proposed two possible policy recommendations as a result of its deliberations. Both policies included a ban on reproductive cloning, which was unanimously supported by the council. The majority of the council proposed a four-year ban on therapeutic cloning while the minority felt that therapeutic cloning would be acceptable if monitored closely and kept within certain acceptable limits. The minority view argued that there is a potential for considerable benefit in exploring the biology of cloning. Since the submission of this report, the U.S. Congress has taken up the debate, but only the House of Representatives has passed a ban; the Senate has not, and so no laws have been enacted regarding human cloning.

The United Nations debated human cloning for four years. In 2004, there were two resolutions before the General Assembly: the Costa Rican resolution, supported by 62 countries including the United States, called for a complete worldwide ban on both reproductive and therapeutic cloning, while another proposal from Belgium, supported by 22 countries, would only ban reproductive cloning. Neither of these resolutions passed. However, in 2005 the

U.N. was able to pass a non-binding resolution calling on world governments to ban all forms of human cloning. This resolution was supported by 84 countries. There were 34 countries against the resolution and 37 abstentions. Individual countries are making their own policies about how and whether human cloning should be used. South Korea, Belgium, China, and Britain have decided that therapeutic cloning will be permitted. Within the United States, the decision is being made at the state level. States such as California and New Jersey permit therapeutic cloning and will benefit from state funding. Many other states are considering similar policies for several reasons. There is a strong feeling that therapeutic cloning will lead to dramatic treatments for disease, but there is also the realization that successful development of therapies from this technology will lead to highly profitable businesses. States need to consider their economies, and therapeutic cloning may provide some states with substantial tax income. Does this not echo the motivation of Dr. Antinori and Dr. Zanos, whose motives we may have criticized earlier? Financial issues are important considerations for a government and must be examined carefully. If a state does not have moral concerns about therapeutic cloning, why not benefit from permitting it? Some states assert a moral obligation to permit therapeutic cloning to relieve human suffering, while others assert that it is morally wrong to permit human cloning. We live in a large, diverse country and should not be surprised to see that we are divided on issues such as human cloning.

CONNECTIONS

It is very likely that someday there will be some form of human cloning, either for purposes of isolating human embryonic stem cells for use in therapeutics or to clone a living person. We have been pumped full of horrific visions of a world with human clones. It is important to sift through these fictional accounts and consider what it would really be like to have human clones among us. Luckily, we have identical twins to turn to for clues. If we ever do clone humans, the most important fact to keep in mind is that no matter where a human comes from or how a human is born, we all have the same rights and should all be treated with the same dignity. There is never any justifiable reason to treat a person badly because he or she is somehow different from us.

FOR MORE INFORMATION

For more information about the concepts discussed in this chapter, search the Web using the following keywords:

In vitro fertilization, Reproductive cloning, Therapeutic cloning, Eugenics, Human cloning

5

Stem Cell Research

WHY ALL THE FUSS ABOUT STEM CELLS?

Scientists and physicians predict a wide variety of wondrous therapeutic uses for human embryonic *stem cells* (hES cells), but since 2001, no federal support has been available in the United States for research to discover these uses. Embryonic stem cells may be able to grow new organs for transplantation, or to repair damaged tissues such as heart muscle affected by heart attacks or brain tissue after strokes. It may be possible to use stem cells to repair spinal cord injuries, to create replacement skin for burn patients, or to treat conditions such as arthritis. Embryonic stem cells may help cure immune disorders or make it possible to correct genetic diseases in patients. These cells may one day even be used for hair and tooth replacement. But no one can yet be sure that these uses will be possible; research and development is needed first to unlock the potential of stem cells.

Scientists are certain that stem cells will make many very significant contributions to science and medicine by expanding our understanding of how life works. This includes better understanding of the events within a cell at the beginning of life, of how embryonic cells develop into adult cells, and of genetic events that control growth and development. Studying stem cells will help us better understand how healthy and unhealthy babies develop, as well as how to avoid problems affecting the unhealthy ones. Stem cells have a great deal to teach us.

However, the discovery of hES cells and the question of using them for research has generated significant public controversy. Even with all the promise these cells offer, ethical and religious questions require consideration because some types of stem cells are harvested by destroying human embryos that are 4–7 days old.

In the United States, this debate has become hotly politicized. In 2001, President George W. Bush announced a complete ban on federally funded hES cell research, with the exception of work on 78 previously established human embryonic stem cell lines. Human embryonic stem cell research later became a major issue in the 2004 presidential campaign, with most Democrats and many Republicans supporting the use of hES cells for medical research while President Bush and many religious groups opposed it. Ron Reagan, the son of former Republican President Ronald Reagan, along with the former president's wife, Nancy Reagan, vocally supported stem cell research. They support stem cell research largely because former President Reagan suffered and finally died from Alzheimer's disease, which may someday be treatable using stem cell–based therapeutics. Ron Reagan's support for stem cell research was so enthusiastic that he gave a speech at the 2004 Democratic National Convention strongly urging Americans to vote for the Democratic presidential candidate, Senator John Kerry, because Kerry would support federal funding for human embryonic stem cell research.

During the same election, California, headed by Republican Governor Arnold Schwarzenegger, was the first state to vote to provide public funding for human embryonic stem cell research. This action overrides the federal ban on funding for human embryonic stem cell research within California and may lead to dramatic medical advances that could be very profitable for California. Other states are following California's lead by also funding human embryonic stem cell research in order to to circumvent the federal ban. These states believe that they are helping develop important new medical breakthroughs for the public as well as ensuring that they will benefit from the huge profits that could come from stem cell technology.

In 2004, President Bush was re-elected, and the federal ban on funding for human embryonic stem cell research remained in effect. To complicate matters, shortly after the 2004 elections, it was announced that the 78 human embryonic stem cell lines that President Bush approved for use in research had been contaminated with mouse molecules and therefore are unusable for developing human therapies.

Given the potential of human embryonic stem cells to decrease human suffering, the debate concerning the ethical use of these cells for research raises the question of whether it would be moral to use embryonic stem cells for research even if a human embryo is destroyed to create them. If it is deemed morally acceptable to use hES cells, this technology may be used to end great suffering. But if it is not morally acceptable to use hES cells, what needs to be done to stop this line of research?

WHAT ARE STEM CELLS?

All the cells in our bodies arise from an original fertilized egg known as the **zygote**. This zygote continues to divide, producing more cells with each round of cell division. Most of these cells specialize and become the tissues that make all of the specific parts of the developing **fetus**. But some of the cells retain the flexibility to become any type of cell in the body. These cells act as a reservoir that provides new cells to replace those lost to tissue damage or age. At the earliest stage of human development, these cells are known as **embryonic stem cells** (**ESC**). These cells are at the heart of the stem cell controversy because a human embryo is the source of these cells.

Stem cells can be found in everyone, young and old. They are cells with the potential to grow into a variety of specialized or **differentiated** cells that our bodies need. Whenever growth or healing occurs in our bodies, stem cells provide the new cells that are needed. Stem cells have the ability to divide, producing two daughter cells; one may remain a stem cell, while the other transforms into whatever cell type our body requires at that time. However, some stem cells are more versatile than others. It seems that the closer a stem cell is to being an embryonic cell, the greater its potential to change into any other type of cell the body needs. More specialized stem cells, like those found in adults, can only become a limited number of cell types, but stem cells from an embryo or fetus are much more versatile. The older stem cells are referred to as **adult stem cells** and the earliest ones are referred to as embryonic stem cells. There are also **fetal stem cells** harvested from fetal tissues like **placenta** or fetal blood. These cells have a greater potential to become other cell types than adult stem cells, but less potential than embryonic stem cells.

Embryonic stem cells are harvested from a very early-stage embryo. After fertilization of an ovum by a sperm, the zygote is formed (see Figure 5.1). The zygote begins to divide after about 30 hours and, within 3–4 days, becomes a mass of approximately 12 cells known as a **morula**. During the next three days, the cells in the morula continue to divide, and for the first time, begin to differentiate into distinct cell types. As this occurs, the cells form a hollow sphere called a **blastocyst**. The blastocyst is composed of about 100 cells that form the **trophoblast**, an outer wall, and an **inner**

Two-cell   Four-cell   Eight-cell   Compacted morula   Blastocyst

Inner cell mass

Blastocoel

Trophoblast

Figure 5.1 This scanning electron micrograph (magnified 14,000 times) captured a sperm fertilizing an egg (top). After the egg has been fertilized, it starts to grow and divide. The process by which a single fertilized egg becomes a blastocyst is illustrated at the bottom.

cell mass that is composed of a group of about 30 cells. These 30 cells are the stem cells with the greatest potential to become any type of cell in the body, and they are known as **totipotent** stem cells.

If the **undifferentiated** inner mass cells are harvested from the 4–7-day-old embryos, these 30 or so cells can be grown in culture in an undifferentiated state into large numbers of embryonic stem cells. They can also be stored frozen for long periods of time. This means that relatively few embryos are needed to create large numbers of cultured stem cells for research and therapeutic use, making it unnecessary to destroy large numbers of embryos.

Once past seven days, the cells from the inner cell mass of an intact embryo begin to differentiate into the three major tissue types of the body: the **ectoderm**, the **mesoderm**, and the **endoderm** (Figure 5.2). Another group of specialized cells become the germ cells. These cells will become the reproductive cells used to produce sperm or ovum for the next generation. At this point, the cells of inner cell mass have started to lose their potential to differentiate. Once these cells have developed into one of the three major tissue types, they may still remain stem cells, but they can no longer become cells of either of the other two major tissue types. From this point on, these stem cells have a limited potential to become any other cell type. In other words, if a stem cell differentiates into an ectodermal stem cell, it can only divide to form ectodermal tissues. It will no longer be able to become a tissue that arises from the mesoderm or endoderm.

This irreversible differentiation happens to all stem cells as they mature. Once stem cells start down a path of differentiation into a particular cell type, they cannot become totipotent stem cells again, nor can they become any other type of cell. Scientists hope that someday they may learn how to create totipotent stem cells from differentiated cells, but so far it is not possible. This means to have stem cells with the greatest potential to differentiate into the greatest number of other cell types, the stem cells must

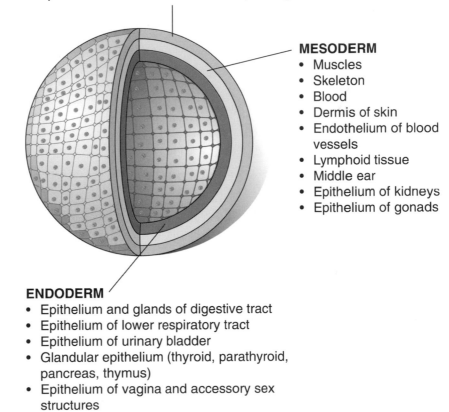

ECTODERM
- Epidermis of skin (including hair, nails and sweat glands)
- Entire nervous system
- Lens, cornea, eye muscles (internal)
- Internal and external ear
- Epithelium of mouth, nose, salivary glands and anus
- Tooth enamel (in mammals)
- Epithelium of adrenal medulla and pineal gland

MESODERM
- Muscles
- Skeleton
- Blood
- Dermis of skin
- Endothelium of blood vessels
- Lymphoid tissue
- Middle ear
- Epithelium of kidneys
- Epithelium of gonads

ENDODERM
- Epithelium and glands of digestive tract
- Epithelium of lower respiratory tract
- Epithelium of urinary bladder
- Glandular epithelium (thyroid, parathyroid, pancreas, thymus)
- Epithelium of vagina and accessory sex structures

Figure 5.2 The inner mass cells of the blastocyst differentiate into the three major tissue types of the human body. The three types of embryonic tissue (ectoderm, mesoderm, and endoderm) are shown here along with the tissues that develop from these layers.

be as close to being inner mass cells as possible. These cells have the greatest potential for therapeutic use, but they also raise the greatest ethical concern.

POTENTIAL APPLICATIONS AND CURRENT SUCCESSES USING EMBRYONIC STEM CELLS

The ability of embryonic stem cells to differentiate into all the cell types of the body, as well as to renew themselves each time they divide, gives them great potential for science and medicine. Scientists predict that embryonic stem cells will someday be a powerful therapeutic tool for replacing diseased, damaged, or worn-out tissues and organs in the human body. This prediction is primarily based on research conducted during the past few decades, using embryonic stem cells from mice. Promising results from these experiments have shown that under the right conditions, the mouse embryonic stem cells can differentiate into any tissue found in an adult mouse. Notable therapeutic successes in mice using mouse embryonic stem cells include treating diabetes and Parkinson's disease, repairing damaged heart tissue, and repairing spinal cord injuries (Figure 5.3).

In humans, there has also been success with stem cell thera-peutics, though not yet with embryonic stem cells. Human adult stem cells have been used to treat human blood diseases such as **leukemia** and **lymphoma** for over 40 years. The cells used for this treatment are called adult **hematopoietic stem cells** (Figure 5.4). These cells are found in the blood and bone marrow of adult humans and are easily isolated. The patient's own adult stem cells or cells from a matched donor can be used. There are types of cancer treatments that kill the blood-forming stem cells in the cancer patient. This is the main objective of the therapy in leukemia and lymphoma. After the treatment is complete, these patients may be unable to replace their own blood cells. When the hematopoietic stem cells, either the patient's own previously frozen cells or cells

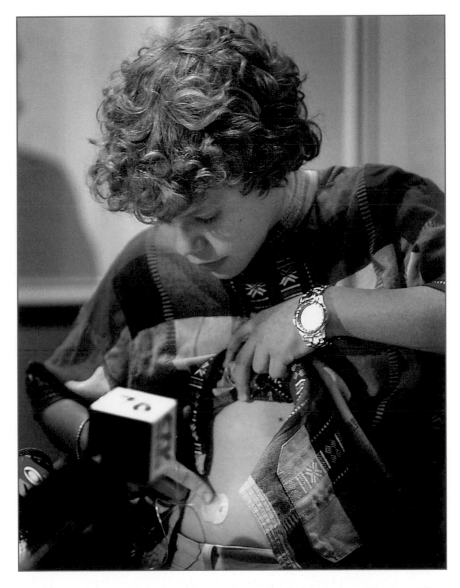

Figure 5.3 Stem cell research has the potential to help patients with diabetes, cancer, spinal cord injuries, and other disabling conditions. In this photograph, 12-year-old Bryan Coble demonstrates how he currently receives his diabetes medication through an insulin pump during a press conference on the Maryland Stem Cell Research Act of 2005.

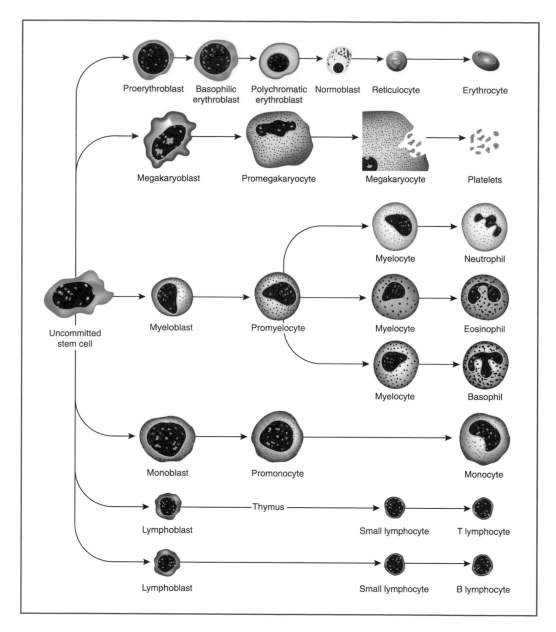

Figure 5.4 Hematopoietic stem cells arise from the bone marrow and differentiate into all of the different types of blood cells. Other stem cells, such as those for muscle and liver growth (hepatocyte), can be found in the liver.

from a matched donor, are introduced into these patients, the stem cells are able to locate the bone marrow, proliferate, and grow. The cells are also able to reestablish the patient's ability to make healthy new blood cells for themselves. But these hematopoietic stem cells are very far along in their own differentiation and so only have the ability to become blood cells. They cannot replace muscle or other body tissues.

Research with humans has also been conducted using a variety of other types of stem cells beside the hematopoietic stem cells. But all this research has been with cells that are more differentiated than embryonic stem cells, so they are less versatile. Nonetheless, promising results have been demonstrated. A small number of patients have been treated for diseases such as diabetes, Parkinson's, and kidney cancer, with some measure of success. The most dramatic announcement came in the fall of 2004 when Korean scientists announced that a woman who had been paralyzed for 19 years was able to walk with the aid of a walker one month after stem cells isolated from umbilical cord blood were injected into her spinal cord. Other therapeutic uses for stem cells that have met with some success include treatment of liver disease and lupus. However, most of these attempts have not led to such dramatic results as those seen in using hematopoietic stem cells in cancer patients. Still, the results strengthen the claims of scientists who believe that embryonic stems cells will someday provide powerful new medical treatments.

As we have seen, researchers predict that the most promising therapeutic developments will come from using human embryonic stem cells. The research using human embryonic stem cells began only in 1998 when these cells were first isolated and cultured by James Thomson and his colleagues. But federal funding restrictions in the United States have slowed this research significantly. In 2001, embryonic stem cell research was limited by President George W. Bush to the 78 preexisting stem cell lines. Since then, no new cell lines have been created and no additional human embryos have been destroyed by publicly funded research efforts. Unfortunately, of the original 78 embryonic stem cell lines, only 22 have been made available for research because of technical difficulties and, as mentioned earlier, all of these may prove unusable because of contamination with mouse proteins. This happened because the original 78 human embryonic stem cell lines were kept alive using mouse "feeder" cells to provide nutrients that cells in culture require. As a result, mouse molecules were accidently transferred to the human embryonic stem cells.

ETHICAL ISSUES ABOUT USING EMBRYONIC STEM CELLS

Two divergent interests define the ethical questions surrounding embryonic stem cell research: pursuing medical research to develop important therapeutics versus respecting and preserving human embryonic life. As a nation, we must address these two concerns to develop a policy that reflects our values and helps us to be a moral society.

Because of the great medical and research potential of human embryonic stem cells, the most desirable course of action would allow us to satisfy both these moral interests. To accomplish this, scientists have sought to create cells with the same properties as embryonic stem cells by means other than the destruction of a 4–7-day-old embryo. The President's Council on Bioethics, which is charged with considering ethical issues related to embryonic stem cell research, has shown considerable interest in this kind of a compromise. However, so far this technology has only been proposed and is not yet possible. Further, any alternative method of creating stem cells is likely to present its own set of ethical considerations that will need to be addressed.

Stop and Consider

What are some possible ways that a diverse population of people like that of the United States can reach an acceptable decision on a topic like stem cell research?

In the absence of an acceptable substitute for embryonic stem cells, it is necessary to explore moral arguments that support or ban their use. What exactly are these arguments? Can we find a moral position acceptable to most people, or will our society remain permanently polarized?

ARGUMENTS FOR AND AGAINST USING EMBRYONIC STEM CELLS FOR RESEARCH

A principal issue in this discussion concerns when an embryo or a fetus achieves full status as a human. This discussion is closely related to abortion issues and has been largely influenced by the long-standing debate about whether or not abortion is moral and should remain legal. Personal opinions about abortion have had a significant effect on people's attitudes about the use of embryonic stem cells for research or therapy. To help us understand why one person may support human embryonic stem cell research while another objects, we need to understand arguments for and against abortion. In examining the arguments of advocates who are against abortions, one can see why they would also object to using human embryos to create stem cells. These individuals hold the view that human life and human rights begin at the moment of conception. This means that the embryo is entitled to the same "right to life" as any other human already born. They believe that this right to life must be legally protected at any stage of life. For these advocates, this makes abortion under any circumstances legally and morally the same as murder. The most ardent supporters of this view consider abortion to be murder and oppose it even if the pregnancy poses a danger to the mother's health or welfare, and in a case when the pregnancy is the result of rape or incest. Protecting the life of the helpless unborn child is seen as the primary moral responsibility. Since creation of embryonic stem cells currently requires the destruction of the embryo, these people view the procedure as an immoral act of murdering the unborn, and so oppose human embryonic stem cell research on these beliefs.

In 1973, the United States Supreme Court ruled, in the land-mark decision known as *Roe v. Wade*, that a fetus is not a person and does not have the same rights as a person who has been born. Since that time, women in the United States have had the right to seek a legal abortion. The mother's rights to control her own body were, by law, placed above the rights of the embryo or fetus. Before that time, women seeking to end an unwanted or untimely pregnancy had to do so in secret. This often placed the woman's life in danger because of the questionable methods used to achieve the abortion and the secrecy that surrounded abortions.

Anti-abortion activists often use the term *pro-life* for their position. Anti-abortion supporters view *Roe v. Wade* as an immoral decision and have worked very hard to have it reversed. Their efforts have recently led to the passage by the U.S. Congress of a ban on late-term abortions, which are known as **partial-birth abortions**. The ban, signed by President Bush in 2003, does not permit a late-term abortion even when the pregnancy poses a risk to the mother's health. However, data suggests that these types of abortions are rarely, if ever, per-formed to protect the physical health of the mother. Supporters of the ban therefore claim that the ban will not have a negative impact on any mother's health. The passage of this ban and the continued efforts by anti-abortion activists illustrate their commitment to their moral beliefs and their resolve to protect unborn human life.

As soon as the public became aware of human embryonic stem cell research, anti-abortion supporters immediately voiced their view that the research was immoral and should not be pursued. Since then, they have been an active political force in shaping the United States' policy toward human embryonic stem cell research. The 2001 ban on federal funding for human embryonic stem cell research resulted largely from their political influence on President Bush and his administration.

Additional concerns voiced by those against using human embryos for research include fear that aborted fetuses could be exploited or commoditized. In other words, women could be paid to get pregnant and abort their fetuses for medical research or for commercial purposes. To address this concern, national policies were adopted in 1993 that protect all fetuses equally, even those that are to be aborted. These policies state that there is never to be any financial incentive for a woman to become pregnant so she can abort a fetus. Further, a woman must have already decided to have an abortion before a request can be made of her to use the fetal tissue for research. Another concern was that research involving human embryonic or fetal tissue would cause an increased abortion rate in the United States. However, no data since abortions became legal in 1973 supports this concern.

Religious beliefs also play an important role in the debate over human embryonic stem cell research. For example, like the anti-abortion supporters, the Catholic Church stated in its *Declarato de Abortu Procurato* (1974) that a human individual is created from the moment of union of the **gametes** and that this newly created person has the same rights as any other living person. The position of the Catholic Church is that knowingly harming the embryo is a gravely immoral and unjustifiable act, even if the motivation is to protect a mother's health or to accomplish good for society.

Other religions view the beginnings of life differently. Many Jewish, Muslim, Unitarian, and Humanist groups support embryonic research and do not consider harvesting stem cells an immoral act. These groups do not view an embryo in the earliest stages as having the same rights as a fully formed human. Instead, developmental milestones such as the beginning of a heartbeat, the ability to live outside the mother, and the ability to perceive pain may be viewed as the time when the embryo becomes a person with full rights. In Jewish tradition, the fetus becomes fully human 40 days after conception. Until then, the fetus is considered part of the woman's body and is only recognized as having full rights independent of its mother at 40 days after conception. Until 1869, the Catholic Church held this same belief.

In Jewish tradition, it is viewed as sinful to harm oneself needlessly. Since the fetus is considered a part of its mother, abortion is prohibited because it is seen as harming the mother. But in cases where the pregnancy will harm the mother, abortion becomes required. In these cases, it is the woman's responsibility to seek treatment and take necessary steps to protect her health. If this means an abortion is required for the mother's health, then an abortion is considered acceptable and necessary. Jewish law does not give an embryo any legal status at all until it is implanted into a mother's womb. When egg and sperm are mixed together in a petri dish during IVF procedures, these embryos are not considered part of a human life unless implanted. The traditional Jewish belief that it is a person's responsibility to strive to find ways to reduce human suffering means that if human embryonic stem cells offer hope to cure terrible diseases, then it is just and necessary to pursue that research. It would be going against God's wishes to neglect the promise of human stem cell therapeutics and allow human suffering to continue.

Stop and Consider

List all the people or groups of people who should have a say in making the decision on stem cell research. Who deserves to have a voice? Should some people's opinions count more than others? Why or why not?

The Islamic view is very similar to the Jewish view except that most Muslims believe that a fetus becomes a human 120 days after conception. At this point, abortion is no longer acceptable except to save the mother's life. Further, in Islam if a fetus is created by

IVF, then the embryo is in an artificial environment and therefore the embryo is not considered a human being and can be used for research without violating religious laws. On the other hand, a fetus in a woman's womb should not be used for research. Based on these beliefs, most Muslim scholars agree that stem cell research is permissible and is most likely a duty if the research could lead to saving lives and reducing human suffering.

Humans almost universally share the idea that we have a moral obligation to help those who are suffering. Most people agree that we should strive to help one another when we can. People opposed to human embryonic stem cell research because it requires the destruction of an early human embryo want to end human suffering just as much as those who support this research; the difference lies in their views concerning the earliest stages of human life.

Another approach that can help us examine the morality of human embryonic stem cell research is to ask how we as a society currently treat embryos. In the United States, no laws currently prohibit embryonic stem cell research. The only ban is on using federal funds for the research. Private companies or foundations may carry out the research at their own expense. However, profit-seeking is the primary motivation for research in the private sector, which means that research may be directed toward efforts with the greatest promise of profit. Medical concerns primarily affecting the underprivileged, who have little money to spend on health care, will be ignored. Discoveries will be patented and possibly withheld from the public to ensure that the companies who invest in research get the greatest return on their investments. Inequities will likely appear in the use of this technology, leading to the benefits being primarily available to the wealthy. In a capitalist economy, businesses are not necessarily expected to act as moral agents. To balance this tendency, public funds are used to support research that addresses the needs of the entire society, not just the privileged.

Individual states, including California, New Jersey, Connecticut, New York, Florida, Wisconsin, Maryland, and several others, are providing public funds for human embryonic stem cell research. They are doing this to assure that the state benefits from potentially valuable discoveries, but also because they feel stem cell research holds so much promise to end suffering. In other countries, public funding of human embryonic stem cell research is already available. The consequence of other countries developing a technology that was first discovered in the United States will be that these other countries will determine how the technology is used and will gain the greatest benefits from commercializing these discoveries. The United States may fall behind and we may be forced to buy technology that we originally developed from foreign countries. This may further add to our growing trade deficit, which harms our country's economy. Perhaps we should be asking if it is in our best national interest to be withholding public funds for this promising research.

Abortion is legal in the United States. States can, however, individually impose restrictions on late-term abortions, but these restrictions must never compromise the health of the pregnant mother. These laws define how our society has chosen to address the issue of human rights for embryos. While women have the legal right to terminate a pregnancy during the early stages, scientists are not permitted to use early-stage embryos to seek new medical therapies. Further, fetal tissue can be used for research with a mother's consent, but embryonic cells cannot be used. Some argue that this situation is moral hypocrisy that ignores our country's established laws. Related to this contradiction is the question of what to do with thousands of unwanted embryos created each year for infertile couples through *in vitro* fertilization (IVF). Typically, a couple has 12 artificially fertilized embryos created, but only a few of these will be implanted. If a successful pregnancy results, something must be done with the surplus embryos. The couple is currently given three choices: have the embryos frozen for future use at considerable expense that includes a fee of around a $100 per month; donate the embryos to another couple seeking to have children; or have the embryos destroyed, which is the most common choice. Each year, thousands of unwanted embryos are destroyed as a result. Many moral questions arise from this practice, if one believes that human rights begin upon conception. To act in accordance with that belief, every one of the fertilized embryos would have to be gestated in a woman's womb and brought to birth. These children would have to be raised and cared for. In light of this dilemma, there are groups that feel IVF should be discontinued as a means for permitting infertile couples to have children.

A fourth possibility for couples who no longer want the unused embryos is to donate them to research. In the past, this was a popular choice. Many couples are comforted knowing that while their embryos can never become children, they may somehow help humanity. Each embryo has the potential to contribute useful cells or information that may help society address medical issues. This view is further supported by our society's practice of using the bodies of deceased people for research and as a source of useful drugs.

Human embryonic stem cell research has not been funded by federal money since 2001, even though more than two-thirds of Americans support embryonic stem cell research for therapeutic uses, as reported by the Juvenile Diabetes Research Foundation in 2004. Some hold that the current ban is the result of the influence of what has been characterized as a primarily ultra-conservative Christian minority view. The United States is becoming more diverse in religious, cultural, and personal beliefs. Many in the scientific and medical community are asking why what appears to be a minority view not shared by the majority of Americans has resulted in the blocking of federal funding for research that has the potential to relieve suffering.

An Advocate for Stem Cell Research

Christopher Reeve (Figure 5.5) was an actor, director, and activist who became paralyzed due to a spinal cord injury he received in a horseback-riding accident in 1995. For the nine years that followed, until his death in 2004, he battled fiercely to overcome his paralysis by seeking every conceivable therapy and treatment. During this time, he campaigned vigorously to advance stem cell research because he believed it held the greatest hope of healing spinal cord injuries in himself and in others. In 1999, Reeve became the Chairman of the Christopher Reeve Paralysis Foundation, a national organization that supports research to develop cures and treatments for paralysis. Until the end of his life, Reeve continued to be as active as possible, directing films and lobbying for funding to pursue stem cell research.

Figure 5.5 Christopher Reeve (1952–2004) is seen here with his wife, Dana, and Jim McGreevy, the former governor of New Jersey. Reeve was a strong advocate for stem cell research, and his legacy continues even after his death.

CONNECTIONS

The debate concerning whether or not the United States will permit the use of federal funds for human stem cell research continues, in light of predictions that stem cell technology may lead to miraculous medical treatments and that humanity may someday benefit from these discoveries. Without a serious investment in research on human ES cells, we will never know their potential and never know if they might have eased the suffering of people like Christopher Reeve or those afflicted with Alzheimer's disease like former President Reagan. Would it be worth the price to cure diseases such as Alzheimer's if in the end we truly believe that we are killing a human being to find the cure? As with other issues, we as educated Americans must make up our minds about this issue. To do this, we must stay informed about the issues we are concerned with. Next, it is up to us to take action if we feel strongly moved by the issue. First, we can accomplish this by voting for officials who represent our beliefs. We can further make a difference by becoming personally active in organizations that represent our point of view. Others may find it effective to write letters to political leaders and to just share their ideas with friends and neighbors. The important point is to actively develop a point of view and then do something to promote it.

FOR MORE INFORMATION

For more information about the concepts discussed in this chapter, search the Web using the following keywords:

Embryonic stem cells, Adult stem cells, Fetal stem cells, Christopher Reeve Paralysis Foundation

6

GM Foods: What Are They Doing to Our Dinner?

GENETICALLY MODIFIED FOODS

Since 1973, when recombinant DNA technology was first introduced, scientists have been able to move genes from place to place within a genome or even from one organism to another unrelated organism. This very powerful technology has led to considerable public debate concerning the morality and safety of using genetic engineering on living organisms. Scientists refer to this ability to move genes as genetic modification (GM) and refer to the plants and animals modified as genetically modified organisms (GMOs). In the last 10 years, recombinant DNA technology has also been used to alter food. There are many possible ways to improve our food using this technology. Some improvements that have already been tried include enhancing the nutritional quality of foods, increasing the productivity of crops and farm animals, and making food production more profitable. But numerous questions need to be asked about using genetic engineering on our foods: Just because we can move genes, is it a good idea? Do we really want to eat GM foods? Is the technology safe? The answers to these questions need to come from both scientific and ethical discussions. Even if GM technology is judged safe, we still must consider people's rights to make personal choices about what they eat (Figure 6.1).

USES OF GM TECHNOLOGY

Genetic modification of plants and animals in a laboratory entails the insertion or removal of genes to achieve a desired outcome. Many genes have already been used and today's plant and animal scientists are proposing and trying new genes at an increasing pace. These genes are selected because they add traits that may improve the plant or animal in some valuable way. Here are examples of how this technology might be or is already being used:

- A human gene could be introduced into a laboratory animal to help study the action of the human gene.

- Animals can be made to grow faster or larger by adding genes for **growth hormones**, making them more productive and profitable.

- Plants can be engineered to be more nutritious.

- Animals can be genetically engineered and bred to produce important drugs in their milk for easy and inexpensive extraction.

- Plants can become pharmaceutical factories, inexpensively producing important new drugs without the danger of possible contamination by animal pathogens.

- Plants that produce edible vaccines can be grown close to the people who require vaccines, eliminating problems of transportation to remote parts of the world.

Figure 6.1 Transgenic rice is one form of genetically modified food. Scientists are working to develop rice that is nutritionally enriched or can grow in unfavorable climates. The plants in these test tubes are cultures of vitamin A-enriched rice.

- **Herbicide**-resistant crops can be grown with fewer applications of chemicals, making them safer to eat, safer for farmers to use, and safer for the environment.

- Insect-resistant crops can be developed that do not need to be sprayed with pesticides.

- Fruit that does not spoil quickly could be shipped to remote places, thereby increasing nutritious food choices for more people.

- Disease-resistant crops and animals can be created to increase production by decreasing losses.

- Drought-resistant plants with the ability to grow in marginal climates could help reduce hunger in those climates.

- Plants can be engineered to remove pollutants from contaminated lands.

This list is not intended to provide all the current or potential uses for GM technology, but to highlight a few of the more promising uses that have made advocates of GM technology so enthusiastic. Since new uses for GM technology are constantly being proposed, it is predicted that using this technology will alter our society and our lives in profound ways. Will these alterations be beneficial or harmful? How can humanity decide whether to allow, limit, or ban GMOs?

BASICS OF GM TECHNOLOGY

Whether you are excited by the promise of using biotechnology to engineer plants and animals or you believe it is dangerous or immoral, it is still important to understand the technology in order to discuss the issues related to GM technology knowledgeably. Like many people, you may not feel you know enough about GMOs to even be sure what you believe about using genetic engineering in plants and animals. However, since this technology is likely to increase in use and increasingly affect our world, genetic engineering deserves serious consideration.

Genetically modified organisms are created in the lab by selecting a desirable trait from one organism, identifying the gene or genes responsible for that trait, and then moving the genes into an organism that will be improved by having the trait. This process sounds simple but is actually very complex and takes years of research and development to achieve.

To illustrate how a GMO organism is created, let's follow the steps used to create insect-resistant corn. For decades, **organic** farmers have been spraying bacteria known as *Bacillus thuringiensis* (Bt) on plants as a safe, organic insecticide. Originally isolated 1901, Bt was found to be the cause of silkworm disease. Later, farmers found that spraying Bt on crops protected the plants from certain insect pests. Bt is not considered a chemical pesticide because it is a naturally occurring bacterium and has been found safe for human consumption. It is therefore considered to be an "organic" pesticide and is currently approved for use in growing organic crops.

Bt kills caterpillars, mosquitoes, and beetle larvae by producing a protein, also known as Bt or Bt toxin, which damages their digestive tracts. In the digestive tract of only certain insects, the Bt toxin binds to specific protein receptors of cells lining the gut. There it damages the cells lining the gut so that they take up too much water and burst, causing the insect to die. Eventually, the insect dies due to bacterial infections. The Bt toxin must be activated by the alkaline digestive tract of insects in order to have its effect. But this insecticidal protein does not harm animals because animals have acidic digestive tracts where the protein is never activated. Animals also lack the cell surface protein receptor that the Bt toxin binds to when it is activated. Bt toxin is therefore harmless to animals and humans.

All proteins like Bt are coded for by genes that are made of DNA. Scientists isolated the gene that codes for the Bt toxin protein and inserted it into a plant to see if the plant could make the Bt toxin, which would make the plant insect-resistant. They also needed to find out if expressing the Bt toxin protein in a plant would harm the plant or those who consume the plant (other than the insects it is designed to kill).

To accomplish this, scientists had to first find the Bt gene in *B. thuringiensis*. It is very difficult to isolate a gene that is just a few thousand DNA **nucleotides** long from a bacterium that has several million nucleotides in its **genome**. This is accomplished by screening tens of thousands to hundreds of thousands of DNA fragments from *B. thuringiensis*. Once isolated, the gene was transferred into embryonic corn cells either by using a gene gun to "shoot" the DNA into the cells or by transforming the cells with a plasmid carrying the gene of interest. These cells were then grown artificially in petri dishes to see if the genes had been inserted in the corn genome and, if so, whether they were in a location that would not cause harmful side effects for the plants (Figure 6.2). Thousands of cultures had to be created and evaluated. The successful cultures were then encouraged to grow into actual corn plants using a combination of specific **plant growth factors**. (Mature plants, capable of being propagated and of producing seeds, can be grown from a few plant cells in culture. Scientists are not able to produce mature animals in laboratory cultures of animal cells.) The seeds from the modified plants then have to be planted and grown. The resulting plants must be tested for insect resistance and for qualities that make the plant a safe and productive source of food. This takes years of growing and cross-breeding genetically modified plants with other varieties of corn until a desirable plant is found that is both insect resistant and agriculturally useful. A few of the thousands of genetically modified plants that were originally created may eventually be judged useable. These plants are commercialized and sold to farmers for planting. To get to this point may require five to seven years of research and development from a team of hundreds of scientists.

Modifying organisms is a very complex, expensive, and time-consuming process. It is not done in haste or without careful consideration. Corporations or research groups that try to create a GM plant or animal spend considerable effort planning and discussing the effort before expending resources. That is why whenever genetic modification is attempted, the resulting organism must be better than the original, possessing a new and useful trait, as well as being judged safe to use and consume. A great deal of planning by intelligent thinkers is required to accomplish genetic modifications.

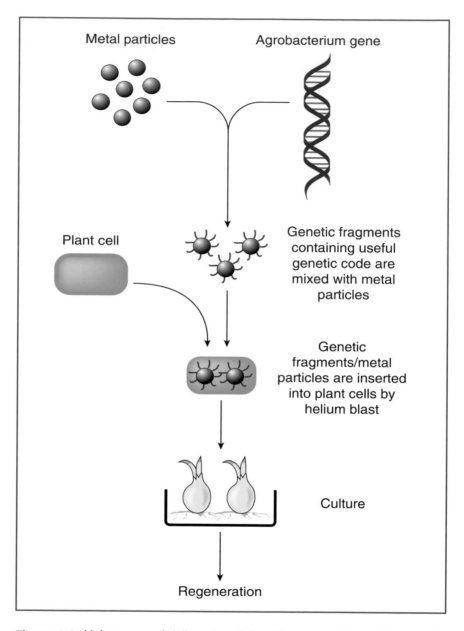

Figure 6.2 Using a special "gun" to "shoot" a gene attached to metal particles is one way to get a desired gene into a cell. The process is illustrated here.

We should not make the mistake of believing that people are just moving genes around at random to see what happens. It is not a casual or haphazard effort.

ETHICAL QUESTIONS CONCERNING GMOS

There are various reasons why people are concerned about GM technology. There are groups opposed to creating GMOs because they believe that GM organisms may be dangerous to eat or harmful to the environment. These people voice fears that moving genes from one organism to another might harm us or our world in unforeseen ways. They express the belief that the complex web of life should not be tinkered with or altered because it is too risky for humans to interfere with natural relationships that have taken eons to evolve in nature. Others feel that altering plants and animals through genetic engineering should not be performed by humans because only "mother nature" or a "divine being" or "divine force" should have the authority to alter life in such fundamental ways. There are also those who believe that the development of GM technology is motivated by the enormous profits that may come from using this technology. They believe that these profit-seekers are not particularly concerned about improving agriculture for the benefit of society, as they claim, but are instead concerned with maximizing profit at any cost to humanity or the environment. There are also those who fear that the risk is too great that GM technology might be used for harmful purposes such as biowarfare and thus should not be further developed or used.

Supporters of GM technology counter with compelling reasons why this technology should be used. They predict that GM technology could improve the quality and amount of food so that starving people in today's world would have enough to eat. Supporters also claim that GMOs can be safe for consumers and the environment when used wisely and carefully. If some or most of the exciting predictions for using GM technology are realized, the results could improve living conditions worldwide. Advocates of GM technology feel that blocking its use is immoral and harmful because doing so would deny these benefits to humanity.

PRO or CON?

Many ethical issues surround the development and use of genetically modified organisms. On one side of the argument are supporters of GMO research, people who believe that genetically modified organisms can help to solve the problem of famine throughout the world and increase health by producing more nutritious foods. Then there are people who are against GMO foods and fear that these novel organisms will harm the environment or that people will use them in dangerous or immoral ways. Finally, there are people who are unsure and sit right in the middle and may agree with some points from each side and disagree with others. Where do you stand on the issue of GMOs?

The debate concerning the safety and wisdom of using GM technology needs to be addressed seriously because there is the potential for great benefit or great harm to come from this technology. We just don't know yet. In light of this uncertainty, society would be wise to confront these issues swiftly, directly, and honestly. Imagine the wonderful breakthroughs if the predictions mentioned earlier come to pass. We cannot morally defend a position that deliberately permits human suffering if we have the ability to safely end that suffering. On the other hand, if the technology is risky and dangerous to people and the environment, then there is the moral responsibility to regulate or block the use of GM technology.

Scientific inquiry offers an effective way to address the issues of GMO safety and its impact on the natural world. Through unbiased scientific investigation, we can find out how well the technology works and its potential applications. Scientists can carry out experiments that test concerns, followed by debates on the significance of their findings. In the scientific community, scientists often disagree and debates can continue for years. In most cases, consensus eventually prevails. As more data becomes available, GM technology will either be deemed safe or rejected as unsafe. Alternatively, it could be found that some uses are acceptable and others are not.

There are also those ethical concerns related to GMOs that address whether this technology should be used at all even if it is proven to be safe to use. Scientific inquiry may ultimately prove GM foods safe for human consumption and for the environment, but society might still reject the use of GM technology based on moral concerns. On the other hand, GM technology may be full of risks, and society might judge that the benefits outweigh the risks. In this case, society would have decided that it is willing to live with the long-term consequences in order to enjoy the short-term benefits. However, either of these positions should only be adopted through intense public debate and not by a small group of people who stand to gain from the outcome.

Below is a list of commonly asked questions regarding GMO use, followed in parentheses by the types of discussion that address the questions being asked.

a) Does creating GMOs go against nature or against God's wishes? (Religious)

b) Is it morally acceptable to genetically modify an organism? (Religious, ethical, and philosophical)

c) How great a chance it there that GM technology will prove harmful? (Scientific)

d) Is it wise to risk using GM technology, given our current level of understanding of the technology? Should the public have a say about their willingness to take the risk? (Ethical and an issue of informed consent)

e) Should GMO products be labeled so that the public can choose to use them or not? (Ethical, economic)

f) What risk to the natural environment is acceptable if we can feed hungry people? (Ethical)

g) How much profit is acceptable when selling GMOs to farmers and consumers? (Ethical, economic)

h) If the GM technology is found to have harmful side effects, who will be responsible for correcting the problem? (Ethical, economic, political)

i) Can the world reach consensus on whether or not GMOs should be created and used? (Ethical, political)

j) Who protects the public interest and can these people be trusted to carry out their responsibilities effectively? (Ethical, scientific, political)

Does Creating GMOs Go Against Nature or Against God's Wishes?

The answer to this question depends on each person's beliefs and worldview. The answer varies from one person to the next depending on influences such as religion, upbringing, education, knowledge of science, exposure to news and entertainment media, as well as the beliefs of others in their community or social group.

Many answer this question with an emotional reaction to GM technology that is influenced by their exposure to the media, religious leaders, friends, family, and teachers. The validity and strength of this type of personal view must be acknowledged, because in a democratic society these people vote for what they believe in and consume only foods they feel comfortable eating.

However, people answering this question solely from an emotional position may not take into account known facts. Their position may not be scientifically defensible and this may not even matter to them. For these people, the potential harm or benefit of GMOs is secondary to their more basic religious or spiritual beliefs. To complicate matters further, a considerable amount of conflicting "factual" information is presented to the public concerning GMOs. As a result, even people who want to be scientific in their thinking must form their opinion based on what they pick and choose to view as factual evidence.

Is It Morally Acceptable to Genetically Modify an Organism?

Does genetic engineering cause unacceptable harm to the modified organism, or if not, is it somehow wrong to manipulate an organism's genes anyway? Based on both ancient and modern teachings, some religions and cultures believe that life is sacred and should not be harmed or manipulated by humans. For these believers, it may never be permissible to harm or alter life. In modern times, this belief has been interpreted to apply to genetic manipulations. But what would strict observance of this principle mean to our day-to-day life? One would expect that this view would prohibit causing harm to any living thing, including the killing and eating of animals. People who believe this are careful to avoid harming any living being.

But let's consider the history of human civilization to determine what is really acceptable to us as humans when it comes to modifying organisms to suit our needs. Humans have caused great changes to nature in their **domestication** of plants and animals. Domestication has been one of humanity's greatest achievements and has had profound effects on plants, animals, and the environment. Has domestication harmed the wild organisms that were altered? If we could ask them, it is very likely that the wild animals would say domestication has caused harm to them in many ways. It has certainly resulted in a loss of freedom for animals to live in the wild and do as they please. In most cases, domesticated plants and animals no longer have the ability to live independent from humans. Their natural instincts have been lost through the process of selective breeding. In some ways, we have enslaved them to our wishes and needs. If, on the other hand, domestication of plants and animals is acceptable in principle because it has allowed humanity to thrive, then does it matter by what method we alter these organisms? Selective breeding sometimes requires confining the animals or forcing them to mate in unnatural ways. Offspring of selectively bred plants and animals are often weak or abnormal. In some cases, these plants and animals must be destroyed. Since domestication and selective breeding have been practiced for over 10,000 years and predates any modern religion, we should be able to agree that humanity has judged this treatment of plants and animals morally acceptable throughout the ages. Virtually everyone benefits and participates in using domesticated plants and animals for food and for our survival. There may be a few humans, such as primitive hunter-gatherer societies or very strict vegetarians, who avoid relying on domesticated plants and animals for their sustenance, but it is virtually impossible to live that way today.

For the general public, GM technology stands apart from selective breeding and domestication because it raises special concerns not associated with selective breeding. For one thing, GM technology is new and mysterious, and when a GM experiment goes wrong or produces an unusual outcome, the public reacts with horror and worries about the spread of genetic mutants. But there is rarely any concern when selective breeding results in an undesirable outcome, which also frequently happens. In fact, we do not usually even hear of these occurrences. People tend not to pay attention to selective breeding issues because the practice has been used for thousands of years. Only farmers and those who work directly in animal or plant breeding know what can go wrong, and they generally accept these nonproductive outcomes as a natural consequence of selective breeding.

Advocates for genetic modifications of plants and animals claim it is a more efficient and predictable way to achieve desirable traits than relying on selective breeding. With selective breeding, two complete genomes are shuffled together and it becomes a matter of chance to get the desired trait expressed in an animal or plant offspring. The genetic changes achieved with selective breeding are accomplished much more slowly, over many generations, and the outcome can never be precisely planned. Using genetic modifications, a desirable trait with known characteristics is intentionally inserted into a particular organism. Therefore, the outcome is generally more controllable and predictable than selective breeding. Through GM technology, very specific traits can be engineered into an organism by design.

Another reason GM technology stands apart from selective breeding is that it provides us with tools to move genes between organisms from different **species** and even between organisms from different kingdoms. This powerful ability worries many people. For example, a trait found in an animal can be engineered into a plant. There was once an attempt to move a gene for protein that protects Artic fish from freezing into strawberries, to protect them from frost damage. The public was worried that this would make strawberries taste like fish. The effort was dropped, but this "antifreeze" protein could not have made strawberries taste like fish because the antifreeze protein is not involved in how fish tastes to us.

(continued on page 120)

Humans and the Domestication of Plants and Animals

Since the birth of agriculture sometime between 10,000 and 12,000 years ago, humans have been altering other life forms by practicing a kind of engineering called selective breeding. Selective breeding is a slow and uncertain process done to alter plants and animals at the genetic level, to make them more valuable to us in some way.

In ancient times, primitive humans fed themselves by hunting and gathering. These people tended to be nomadic, following the food supply. They ate only what nature provided—wild animals, seeds, berries, roots, and greens. Abundance or scarcity of food depended on the weather, the season, and on what animals were in the area. About 10,000–12,000 years ago, this way of survival began to change. Humans found it easier and more productive to capture animals and grow them in captivity, and to plant large crops rather than eating what was found naturally. These ideas and observations were the birth of agriculture. The wild plants and animals were domesticated through a process of selective breeding. Selective breeding occurs when the best plants and animals are chosen to breed the next generation.

Today's farmers spend a lot of time and thought making sure that their plants produce as much food as possible. Ancient farmers were no different. Each year, ambitious farmers saved seeds from the biggest, most desirable plants. The next year they planted these seeds, hoping they would produce a new generation of the better plants. Sometimes this worked and sometimes it did not. Farmers would also carefully cross two plants that each had a trait they judged desirable. This might be a plant that produces more seeds, it might be that the seeds were bigger, or that the plant was not as likely to be eaten by a particular insect or pest. Some of the offspring would display both desirable traits, while others might have one trait or the other. Farmers would collect the seeds from the plants with the best combination of desirable traits and replant them the following year. Over a period of years, farmers could count on increasing numbers of their plants having the desirable traits. Eventually, farmers were able to change plants to be increasingly productive, to taste better, to grow in new climates, to be insect resistant, or to be more nutritious. The foods we eat today result from thousands of years of this sort of selective breeding.

The food crops and farm animals that we are accustomed to seeing and eating are domesticated, not found in the wild. Corn and maize illustrate the difference

Figure 6.3 Over a period of thousands of years, three naturally occurring genetic mutations and much selective breeding by humans was necessary to convert teosinte (on the left), a grass-like plant with numerous tassels and small seed clusters, into the productive corn plant that feeds much of the world today (one kernel shown). Modern corn, or maize, has large ears filled with nutritious kernels. Teosinte is not an abundant food source.

between wild and domesticated food. Where did corn come from and what is it like in its natural or wild form? The corn that we eat and feed to animals is a mutant of a Central American plant called **teosinte** (Figure 6.3), a grass-like plant with numerous tassels and small seed clusters. Teosinte is a plant with tiny seeds that are tedious to harvest and tough to chew. Today's corn has large ears filled with nutritious kernels. Through selective breeding, farmers were able to develop the corn that we know and love to eat today.

grown using chemical pesticides and herbicides, possibly making the GM products safer and purer. They claim that public reluctance to buy GM products because of this misconception would be an unfair economic burden to these companies.

> ### Stop and Consider
> Next time you go to the grocery store, see if you can find any foods labeled as "Genetically Modified" or "Not Genetically Modified." Are any of these foods that you eat regularly? Do you want to know if the food you eat has been genetically modified? Why or why not?

- How much profit is acceptable when selling GMOs to farmers and consumers?

- If the GM technology is found to have harmful side effects, who will be responsible for correcting the problem?

These two questions are about money and responsibility. Businesses could potentially make huge profits with GM technology. Those who stand to benefit may be tempted to maximize profits, and some would do so regardless of consequences to public welfare. But even if GMOs prove safe and even if GM technology can solve food problems for the world's people, how much profit is acceptable? In a capitalist economy, businesses are expected to maximize profits to succeed. This leads some businesses to pursue profit by any means. Can this technology be regulated to avoid exploitation of the consumer? Further, there may be greedy people who try to profit even when a technology is unsafe. Can this be prevented?

Government and regulatory agencies around the world are already monitoring GM technology as they do for many other technologies that affect public welfare, such as in the **pharmaceutical** and energy production industries. These agencies try to ensure "fair and safe" practices while also protecting the public interest. They are prepared to take action if problems develop from the use of GM technology and are expected to ensure that those responsible are held accountable. On the other hand, these agencies are usually under-funded and given limited enforcement power, which hampers their effectiveness. To address this problem, our society has developed a network of consumer advocacy groups (organizations that protect public interest by monitoring the quality of manufactured goods and services) and political activist organizations (groups of people working to influence a particular aspect of public policy) that play a very important role in protecting the public interest. These groups are an example of "checks and balances" in our society. In the case of GM technology, they play an important role in alerting the public to potential dangers and limiting the harm that can result from greedy businesses.

Can the World Reach Consensus on Whether or Not GMOs Should Be Used or Banned?

This question asks who decides whether to permit GM technology. Who has the right to decide if this technology should be used to alter our food? Who can we trust to make an ethically correct choice? Many groups are interested in making this decision for us and see themselves as **stakeholders** because they believe they have something to gain or lose through the GMO debate. These groups include the scientific community, businesses, the public, consumer and political advocacy groups, and governments.

Stop and Consider

Why is the debate associated with the use of GMOs so important? Can you suggest a way that the different sides of the debate can compromise?

As a stakeholder in this debate, and in general, the scientific community can be trusted to care about the impact of their advancements on humanity and the planet. Contrary to media influenced stereotypes of scientists, most are socially responsible, open-minded people who care deeply about improving life through their discoveries. Most scientists are motivated by the rewards of discovery, not by financial reward. Public distrust of scientists is in part justified by past examples of unethical practices by some, but these are rare exceptions in a profession full of people of great character like Albert Einstein, Linus Pauling, Louis Pasteur, Madam Curie, and many others. However, experiments conducted by Nazi scientists in Germany during World War II still horrify people when they learn what was done.

The business community has a lot at stake in the decision to use GM technology. Business ethics can be questionable, as discussed earlier, because of the potential to earn vast profits from GM technology. There is also great pressure in business to move ahead as quickly as possible with profitable new products, which sometimes means that they release a new product before all safety concerns have been addressed. However, not all businesses succumb to this pressure; many work hard to prevent it, and not all businesses put profit above public safety concerns. Many companies fall somewhere in between the extremes by being somewhat public-minded, yet at times willing to bend ethical practices in the name of profit.

Ideally, there would be a national and worldwide consensus concerning whether or not it is safe to use GMOs. Many worldwide agreements have been made to protect humanity. For instance, there is almost worldwide agreement that it is a good idea to limit nuclear weapons to avoid nuclear war and nuclear accidents. There is also general agreement to limit the release of **chlorofluorocarbons** to protect the Earth's **ozone layer** and to reduce carbon dioxide emissions to slow global warming. In principle, if not in practice, all nations agree that these technologies need to be regulated. Even if the agreements are not ironclad and strictly followed by all parties, they do offer some level of security and protection. Some nations will inevitably stray or refuse to participate, but this does not necessarily diminish the powerful statement made by a worldwide agreement. If GM technology is convincingly demonstrated to be harmful to humanity and to the world, then a similar worldwide agreement would be debated and agreed to for GMOs. However, this has not happened so far because there has not been compelling scientific evidence that GM technology is causing great harm. To the contrary, it seems that even governments that have been very slow to accept the use of this technology are cautiously beginning to allow it.

It is always wise to be cautious and base acceptance of new technologies such as GMOs on concrete evidence. Demonstrated caution can strengthen public confidence in a new technology. In the case of GMOs, caution is helping to allay fears that profit, greed, or biased enthusiasm by the scientific community are promoting an agenda of acceptance of GM technology before it is proven safe.

Who Is Protecting the Public Interest and Can They Be Trusted?

This last question is very important. Who protects the public in regard to GM technology and are they reliable? There are currently three regulatory agencies in the United States responsible for monitoring the safety of GMOs: (1) the Food and Drug Administration (FDA); (2) the Environmental Protection Agency (EPA); and (3) the United States Department of Agriculture (USDA). These agencies are expected to impartially examine scientific evidence and decide what is safe and what is unsafe for the public. In general, they do a good job of protecting public interests, and there is usually strong public trust in these agencies. The FDA has, at times, received the highest trust rating of any government agency, but serious concerns occasionally arise about how these agencies make their decisions. Sometimes these agencies clearly make bad decisions that do not protect public safety; sometimes this occurs because of genuine errors in judgment, but documented cases exist in which bad decisions were made because of political and business pressure. There have been cases where outright corruption has influenced decision-making at these agencies. Unfortunately, bad decisions result in loss of public confidence in these agencies, and it can take years before the public is again willing to trust these agencies' judgment or accept new technologies that they approve. It seems logical and beneficial to everyone to ensure that these organizations are not manipulated by outside interests and that they remain independent and objective.

Placing the pursuit of profit before safety is dangerous. Powerful companies and individuals frequently rely on risk assessments used to make decisions concerning products and public safety. Risk assessment is when a company, or some other interested party, asks how many people are likely to benefit and how many are likely to be harmed by an action or decision. If the percentage of people harmed is considered small enough and the profits are large enough, then the product will be made available to the public and sold. Another ethical question one might consider is how many people harmed is too many? Are one, two, ten, a hundred harmed people enough to make the action wrong? And how much profit justifies knowingly harming people? A company is likely to consider how much they might be liable for in a lawsuit if people are harmed or how much insurance they can afford to protect themselves when considering whether to sell a questionable product. This type of thinking by profit-making businesses is one reason why regulatory agencies need to remain unbiased. Only an independent agent that is not pressured by politics or money can make a correct decision when huge amounts of profit are involved.

To relate this question to GM technology, many critics fear that just this sort of risk assessment by large impersonal businesses will be used to make determinations about the safety of GMOs. There is little public trust that businesses themselves make ethical decisions. Further, the public does not believe that regulatory agencies charged with protecting the public interest are strong enough to stand up to the pressure exerted by today's powerful businesses. As a result, many activist groups, such as Greenpeace, the Union of Concerned Scientists, and the Sierra Club, campaign against GM technology. These groups have a wide range of concerns about GMOs, some of which may turn out to be valid and some of which are likely to be unfounded.

One example is the fear that GM corn will kill monarch butterflies. For several years, the monarch butterfly was the symbol of resistance to GMOs because it was feared they were being killed as a result of the use of Bt corn, discussed earlier in the chapter. Laboratory experiments seemed to show a potential that the monarchs would be harmed by the Bt corn used to kill the corn borer worm. Corn borer worm damage to corn plants causes a bigger decrease in crop yield than any other insect pest (Figure 6.4). Using Bt corn also means that fewer chemical pesticides are needed to grow the corn. Makers of Bt corn claim that using the corn is good for the environment because it decreases the need to use harmful chemicals to achieve an abundant harvest. Bt corn is also promoted as being good for farmers, who no longer have to spend time and money on expensive chemical pesticides and are no longer being exposed to highly toxic chemical pesticides. However, researchers realized that monarch butterflies are also sensitive to Bt corn and may be killed if they injest pollen from the Bt corn. But the monarchs do not eat corn plants; instead they feed on the milkweed plant. The fear was that the milkweed plant might become covered with pollen from the Bt corn. There was widespread public outrage and publicity from advocacy groups about this danger to

Figure 6.4 Top: Corn borer worm on an ear of corn. Notice how the worm destroys the corn. Bottom: An adult monarch butterfly. It was believed by anti-GMO activist groups that the Bt toxin found in GM corn pollen would harm these butterflies. It became a national issue to protect these butterflies from the dangers of GM corn until carefully controlled scientific research demonstrated that monarchs are not harmed by GM corn. Instead, it became apparent that other human activities, including global warming, are more to blame for the decline in their population.

the butterflies, and this scenario was frequently publicized as an example of how dangerous GM technology was and how profit-hungry corporations put their interests before that of the public's. Opponents of Bt argued that it should be banned before all the butterflies were killed. However, a couple of years of careful scientific experiments showed that relatively few monarchs are likely to ever be harmed because the butterflies are not feeding when the corn is producing pollen, the pollen is heavy and stays mostly in the cornfields where there are relatively few milkweed plants, and the amount of pollen the butterflies would have to ingest was much higher than amounts found on milkweed plants growing near cornfields. It was further determined that the number of monarchs killed by other human activities, including loss of habitat and colliding with cars each year on the highway, is far greater than the number of the butterflies that might be killed by Bt corn pollen. It is also highly likely that spraying chemical pesticides on the crops, which indiscriminately kills a wide variety of both harmful and beneficial insects, would also have more effect on the monarchs' population than would Bt corn pollen. Since this controversy came to light, close to 80% of eastern monarchs have been killed by another human activity. The loss of their natural habitat in Mexico has forced the monarchs to congregate at higher altitudes where temperatures are lower. As a result, most of the butterflies have been frozen to death. However, few anti-GMO activist organizations continue to be concerned about the welfare of the monarchs.

It is always good practice to question the impact of new technologies on public safety. However, it is important to make claims based on factual concerns rather than biased feelings. There may be significant benefit in using Bt corn. The companies selling the seed corn may benefit from increased profits; the farmer may benefit from decreased use of dangerous chemicals, less labor required to produce the crop, and increased income; and the public may benefit from decreased food costs and decreased harmful environmental effects because fewer chemicals are needed to grow crops. But the example of how quickly public opinion was turned against Bt crops by false claims of harming butterflies shows how easily the public comes to distrust large corporations. Does this distrust result from past unethical practices by big corporations? How should these corporations behave to ensure ethical practices and gain public trust? Corporate management views their primary responsibilities to be maximizing earnings and pleasing investors. Social responsibility may be less important to their business plan than large profits. Is this an ethical position for these companies to take? If so, how can the public be protected?

CONNECTIONS

Great promise and great controversy surround genetically modified organisms. Are they safe? So far, it seems so. Do we want to eat them? The public has very mixed feelings. Many forces are at work, pulling us in both directions: we want to embrace this wonderful new technology and yet we must be cautious not to unleash a terrible horror on our precious planet. However, it is up to us as an informed public and as responsible citizens to choose. If we do not choose, we are giving up our personal power to help make the world a place where we want to live.

FOR MORE INFORMATION

For more information about the concepts discussed in this chapter, search the Web using the following keywords:

GMO, Genetically modified organisms, Bt or *Bacillus thuringiensis*, Teosinte, Organic foods

c. 8000 B.C. Crops and livestock domesticated

c. 4000-2000 B.C. Yeast used to leaven bread and make beer and wine

c. 500 B.C. Moldy soybean curds used to treat boils (first antibiotic)

c. 100 A.D. Powdered chrysanthemums used as first insecticide

1590 Microscope invented

1600 Beginning of the Industrial Revolution in Europe

1663 Cells discovered

1675 Anton van Leeuwenhoek discovers bacteria

1797 Edward Jenner inoculates child to protect him from smallpox

1857 Louis Pasteur proposes microbe theory for fermentation

1859 Charles Darwin published the theory of evolution through natural selection

1865 Gregor Mendel published the results of his studies on heredity in peas

1890 Walther Fleming discovers chromosomes

1914 First use of bacteria to treat sewage

1919 Term *biotechnology* was coined by Karl Ereky, a Hungarian engineer

1922 First person injected with insulin, obtained from a cow

1928 Alexander Fleming discovers penicillin

1933 Hybrid corn commercialized

1944 Oswald Avery, Colin MacLeod, and Maclyn McCarty prove that DNA carries genetic information

1953 James Watson and Francis Crick publish paper describing the structure of DNA

1961 *Bacillus thuringiensis* registered as first biopesticide

1966 Marshall Warren Nirenberg, Har Gobind Korhana, and Robert Holley figure out the genetic code

1973 Herbert Boyer and Stanley Cohen construct first recombinant DNA molecule and reproduce it

1975 First monoclonal antibodies produced

1975 Asilomar Conference held; participants urge U.S. government to develop guidelines for work with recombinant DNA

1977 Human gene expressed in bacteria

1977 Method developed for rapid sequencing of long stretches of DNA

1978 Recombinant human insulin produced

1980 U.S. Supreme Court allows the Chakrabarty patent for a bacterium able to break down oil because it contains two different plasmids

1980 Stanley Cohen and Herbert Boyer awarded first patent for cloning a gene; Paul Berg, Walter Gilbert, and Frederick Sanger awarded Nobel Prize in chemistry for the creation of the first recombinant molecule

1981 First transgenic animals (mice) produced

1982 Human insulin, first recombinant biotech drug, approved by the FDA

1983 Human immunodeficiency virus, the cause of AIDS, is identified by U.S. and French scientists

1983 Idea for PCR (polymerase chain reaction) conceived by Kary Mullis, an American molecular biologist

1984 First DNA-based method for genetic fingerprinting developed by Alec Jeffreys

1985 First field testing of transgenic plants resistant to insects, bacteria, and viruses

1985 Recombinant human growth hormone approved by the FDA

1985 Scientists discover that some patients who had received human growth disorder hormone from cadavers had died of a rare brain disorder

1986 First recombinant cancer drug approved, interferon

1987 The first field test of a recombinant bacterium, Frostban, engineered to inhibit ice formation

1988 Human Genome Project funded by Congress

1990 Recombinant enzyme for making cheese introduced, becoming the first recombinant product in the U.S. food supply

1990 First human gene therapy performed in an effort to treat a child with an immune disorder

1990 Insect-resistant Bt corn approved

1994 First gene for susceptibility to breast cancer discovered

1994 First recombinant food (FlavrSavr tomatoes) approved by FDA

1994 Recombinant bovine growth hormone (bovine somatotropin, BST)

1997 Weed killer–resistant soybeans and insect-resistant cotton commercialized

1997 Dolly the sheep, the first animal cloned from an adult cell, is born

1998 Rough draft of human gene map produced, placing 30,000 genes

1999 Jesse Gelsinger, a participant in a gene therapy trial for an inherited enzyme defect, dies as a result of the treatment

2000 First report of gene therapy "cures" for an inherited immune system defect. A few months later, several of the treated children developed a blood cancer

2002 Draft of human genome sequence completed

2003 First endangered species cloned (the banteng, a wild ox of Southeast Asia)

2003 Dolly, the cloned sheep, develops a serious chronic lung disease and is euthanized

2003 Japanese scientists develop a genetically engineered coffee plant that produces low caffeine beans

2004 Korean scientists report human embryonic stem cell produced using a nucleus from an adult cell

2005 Korean scientists improve success rate of human adult nuclear transfer to embryonic cells by 10-fold

Adult stem cells—Undifferentiated cells found in differentiated tissues of the adult body. These cells can renew the cells of the tissue in which they are found or make copies of themselves. These cells persist for the lifetime of the organism.

Alzheimer's disease—A neurodegenerative disease, usually associated with aging, that leads to loss of mental functions.

Animal husbandry—Breeding and raising animals for agricultural purposes.

Antimicrobial—Agents that can kill microorganisms.

Applied ethics—Use of ethical discussion to determine the morality of current issues or practices.

Biotechnology—Using discoveries in biology to produce useful products and useful organisms. Examples of this technology range from using yeast to make bread to advanced techniques used to sequence the human genome.

Bioweapons—Weapons that use biological material as an agent to cause harm, such as the 2001 anthrax attacks in the United States.

Blastocyst—An early-stage animal or human embryo made of a hollow ball of cells.

Caste—A rigid system of social order usually based on hereditary social divisions.

Chlorofluorocarbons—Chemicals containing carbon, fluorine, chlorine, and hydrogen. These compounds are mainly used as refrigerants and are believed to be responsible for depletion of the Earth's ozone layer, which keeps out harmful ultraviolet rays.

Daughter cells—Cells resulting when a single parent cell divides.

Deoxyribonucleic acid (**DNA**)—Carrier of genetic material that determines inheritance of traits.

Differentiated—When stem cells have changed into cells of a particular tissue type.

DNA—See **Deoxyribonucleic acid**.

Domestication—Taming a wild animal or plant through generations of selective breeding to become a work animal, pet, or food source.

Ebola virus—Highly contagious virus that causes hemorrhagic fever, which is frequently fatal. The virus was first noticed near the Ebola River in the Republic of Congo.

Ectoderm—Outer layer of cells in a developing embryo that gives rise to various tissues, including the epidermis of the skin and the epithelium of the nasal cavity and mouth, as well as the nervous system and eyes.

Embryo—Earliest stages of development of a fertilized animal egg. In humans, this stage lasts from the time when the fertilized egg attaches to the uterine wall of the mother until the eighth week of pregnancy.

Embryonic stem cells (**ESC**)—Cells derived from early-stage embryos that can differentiate into all the cell types found in the adult body.

Emerging diseases—Illnesses caused by organisms that have not been recognized as widespread human pathogens in the past. The increased incidence of these illnesses can be due to newly evolved pathogenic microbes, greater contact between various populations of humans around the world enabling microbes to spread to places where they were not seen before, or due to alteration and disturbance of habitats leading to conditions that favor the growth of pathogens that were uncommon or contained in the past.

Endoderm—Innermost layer of cells in the developing embryo; this layer becomes the gastrointestinal tract, urinary bladder and urethra, and respiratory tract.

Energy metabolism—Process of breaking carbon-carbon bonds in glucose to collect energy for the cell stored in the phosphate bonds of ATP molecules. This energy helps the cell carry out processes necessary for life.

Ethics—Branch of philosophy dealing with morality of human conduct and determination of right and wrong, good and bad.

Eugenics—Selective breeding to encourage improvement of humans or animals. This practice was taken to extremes by Nazi Germany during World War II to justify the extermination of millions of people who were wrongfully said to be genetically inferior. Today, eugenics is associated with racism and discrimination.

Euthanized—Putting an animal or human to death painlessly or allowing death to occur by withholding life-sustaining measures. May be practiced to avoid needless suffering or in cases of incurable disease.

Factor IX—Enzyme in human blood plasma essential to normal blood clotting that may be inactive or missing in some forms of hemophilia.

Fetal stem cells—Primitive cells found in the fetus that can develop into many but not all of the organs of the body.

Fetus—A young animal in the womb or inside an egg. In humans, this stage begins after the second month of gestation.

Fisheries—Place where fish or shellfish are caught or bred. Also used to refer to the industry of catching fish.

Gametes—Reproductive cells that join together to form a new organism. In mammals, these are sperm from the male and the egg or ovum from the female. Each gamete carries half of the normal number of chromosomes; upon union, the newly formed embryo has a full set of chromosomes, half from each parent.

Genetic—Having to do with genes and the genome.

Genetic diversity—Existence of various forms of a particular gene or trait within a species that increase variability within the population and thereby its chances of survival.

Genetic engineering—Ability to manipulate and change the genetic makeup of an organism by altering its DNA.

Genetically engineered—An organism that has had genetic material added or removed in order to alter the organism's phenotype.

Genome—All of the genetic information found in a cell or an organism.

Genotype—Genetic makeup of an organism. All the genes found in an organism as well as the particular form of each gene.

Growth hormones—Chemical factors that signal a cell or organism to grow.

Hematopoietic stem cells—A type of stem cell that can become a red blood cell or any of the various types of white blood cells.

Hemophilia—The oldest known hereditary disorder of blood clotting. The two types of hemophilia are type A and B. Both forms are caused by low levels or the complete absence of proteins essential for blood clotting. Patients with hemophilia A lack a protein known as Factor VIII, and those with hemophilia B lack Factor IX. There are about 20,000 hemophilia patients in the United States.

Herbicide—Chemicals used to kill weeds.

In vitro—literally means "in glass" and refers to experiments performed in a test tube, petri dish, or lab container rather than in a living organism.

In vitro fertilization (IVF)—The process of bringing together an ovum (egg) and a sperm in a medical laboratory. Often used to help couples who are having trouble conceiving by natural means; this procedure can also be used with animals to artificially create a fertilized egg.

Infertile—The inability of a male and female to mate and produce offspring, frequently because of a physical problem in the male or female.

Informed consent—Permission to proceed with a medical procedure or experiment based on clear understanding by the patient or subject of possible outcomes or consequences.

Inner cell mass—A group of 30 or so cells that form on the inside of the developing blastocyst and can be collected as embryonic stem cells. In the intact blastocyst, these cells will differentiate into the three germinal cell types of the developing fetus.

Leukemia—Form of bone marrow cancer leading to an increased level of white blood cells.

Lyme disease—Chronic inflammatory disease caused by a tick-borne spirochete, *Borrelia burgdorferi*; it results in joint pain, fatigue, memory loss, and other neurological symptoms.

Lymphoma—Type of cancer arising from the cells of the lymph nodes.

Mesoderm—Middle layer of embryonic cells that develops into the blood, blood vessels, muscles, and connective tissues.

Microinjection—Use of a very fine, drawn-glass needle small enough in diameter to inject DNA into an intact cell or remove DNA from a cell.

Mitochondrial DNA—Small circular chromosome found in mitochondria. This DNA is 16,500 base-pairs long and contains 37 genes needed for mitochondria to function properly. Other genes needed for mitochondria to function are located on the nuclear DNA of the cell.

Mitosis—The way that non-reproductive eukaryotic cells divide to produce two daughter cells.

Morula—A compact ball of 12 or more cells that forms 3–4 days after a zygote is fertilized.

Nucleotides—Building blocks of DNA and RNA composed of a phosphate group, a five-carbon sugar (ribose or deoxyribose), and a purine or pyrimadine nitrogenous base.

Oocyte—Unfertilized immature animal egg cell.

Organic—Food grown naturally, using compost as fertilizer and other non-chemical methods rather than chemicals to control pests or kill weeds.

Ovum—Female gamete, also known as an egg cell. Plural is *ova.*

Ozone layer—Uppermost tier of the Earth's atmosphere. At 8–30 miles up, this layer filters out harmful ultraviolet light.

Parkinson's disease—A neurodegenerative disease affecting the dopamine-producing neurons of the brain. It is characterized by hand tremors and a shuffling gate.

Partial-birth abortions—Type of late-stage pregnancy termination in which delivery is induced and the fetus is destroyed. May be performed for the mother's health or because of problems with the fetus.

Pathogen—Microorganism that causes disease.

Pesticide—Chemical used to kill insects harmful to humans or agriculture.

Pharmaceutical—Chemical agents used to treat or cure diseases.

Placenta—Organ that forms on the lining of the womb during pregnancy and nourishes the developing fetus.

Plant-growth factors—Molecules that stimulate plant cells to differentiate and become fully developed plants.

Plasmid—Piece of DNA inside a bacterium that is separate from the bacteria's genetic material, but is copied each time the bacterium divides. It is used in biotechnology to introduce new genetic information into a bacterial cell.

Prion—(proteinaceous infectious particle) A misshapen form of a normal cellular protein which has the ability to influence the shape of normal proteins and convert them to the misshapen form. This action leads to degenerative brain disorders in animals and humans.

Recombinant DNA—Insertion of a segment of DNA or a gene into another piece of DNA, either naturally or through laboratory manipulation, resulting in a DNA molecule with a new genetic combination of genes.

Reproductive cloning—Cloning performed to produce a living baby.

Selective breeding—Process of creating domesticated animals or plants with desired traits through controlled mating.

Somatic cell—Any cell from the body of a multicellular organism, excluding the reproductive cells.

Somatic cell nuclear transfer—Process of removing the nucleus from an egg cell and using microinjection or other means to insert the nucleus from a somatic cell to create a cloned embryo.

Species—Organisms that are similar morphologically and genetically and that have the ability to breed productively.

Sperm—Male gamete that fertilizes the female egg. Millions of sperm are produced daily by male humans.

Stakeholders—Group of people with a vested interest in the outcome of a situation or event.

Stem cell—Cell with the ability to differentiate into a variety of other cell types.

Surrogate mother—Woman who agrees to bear a child for someone else by having a fertilized embryo that is not her own implanted into her womb, completing the pregnancy, giving birth, and surrendering the resulting infant to the people who provided the embryo.

Teosinte—Tall grass from Mexico known as *Zea mexicana* that is the ancestral plant of corn or maize.

Teratogenic—Agent that causes developmental deformities.

Therapeutic cloning—Creating genetically identical cells or organisms for the purpose of finding cures or treatments for diseases.

Totipotent—Ability of some stem cells to differentiate into any other cell type of the body.

Transgenic animals—Animals created by inserting a gene from another organism into the fertilized egg so that the gene becomes part of the animal's genome and is expressed in the animal.

Transgenic organism—An organism created when genes from one organism are inserted into another. See also **Transgenic animals**.

Trophoblast—Outer layer of the early embryo surrounding the inner cell mass; this outer layer develops into tissues that later nourish the developing fetus.

Tuberculosis—Infection, primarily of the lungs, caused by *Mycobacterium tuberculosis* and characterized by fever, weakness, coughing, and loss of appetite. If untreated, the disease kills 50% of its victims. It is the most common infectious disease, infecting almost a third of the world's population.

Twinning—Process of splitting an early-stage embryo into separate cells that each have the potential to develop into a separate adult organism. Also known as embryo slitting.

Undifferentiated—Cells that have not yet changed from stem cells into specialized cells of the body.

Vaccine—Preparation of weakened or killed bacteria or virus introduced into the body to stimulate an immune reaction that will protect against the live version of the pathogen.

Vivisection—Practice of dissecting a living organism.

Zygote—A single-celled fertilized egg that results when an egg and a sperm unite.

Barnum, Susan R. *Biotechnology: An Introduction*. Belmont, CA: Wadsworth Publishing, 1998.

Brown, Richard E. *Rockefeller Medicine Men: Medicine and Capitalism in America*. Los Angeles, CA: University of California Press, 1979.

DeSalle, Rob, and Michael Yudell. *Welcome to the Genome: A Users' Guide to the Genetic Past, Present, and Future*. Hoboken, NJ: John Wiley and Sons, 2005.

Eiseman, Elisa. *The National Bioethics Advisory Commission: Contributing to Public Policy*. Santa Monica, CA: RAND, 2003.

Fox, Michael W. *Beyond Evolution*. New York, NY: The Lyons Press, 1999.

Fukuyama, Francis. *Our Post Human Future: Consequences of the Biotechnology Revolution*. New York, NY: Farrar, Straus and Giroux, 2002.

Fumento, Michael. *Bio Evolution: How Biotechnology is Changing Our World*. San Francisco, CA: Encounter Books, 2003.

Gert, Bernard, et al. *Morality and the New Genetics*. Sudbury, MA: Jones and Bartlett Publishers, 1996.

Gold, Michael. *A Conspiracy of Cells*. Albany, NY: State University of New York Press, 1986.

Greek, C. Ray, and Jean Swingle Greek. *Sacred Cows and Golden Geese: The Human Cost of Experiments on Animals*. New York, NY: The Continuum International Publishing Group, 2002.

Heilbroner, Robert L. *The Worldly Philosophers*. New York, NY: Time Inc., 1962.

Hilts, Philip J. *Protecting America's Health: The FDA, Business, and One Hundred Years of Regulation*. New York, NY: Alfred A. Knopf, 2003.

Holland, Suzanne, Karen Lebacqz, and Laurie Zoloth. *The Human Embryonic Stem Cell Debate: Science, Ethics, and Public Policy*. Cambridge, MA: MIT Press, 2001.

Kass, Leon R., ed. *Human Cloning and Human Dignity: The Report of the President's Council on Bioethics*. New York, NY: Public Affairs, 2002.

Kass, Leon R. *Life, Liberty and the Defense of Dignity: The Challenge for Bioethics*. San Francisco, CA: Encounter Books, 2002.

Kenney, Martin. *Biotechnology: The University-Industrial Complex*. New Haven, CT: Yale University Press, 1986.

Kitcher, Philip. *The Lives to Come: The Genetic Revolution and Human Possibilities.* New York, NY: Simon & Schuster, 1996.

Lambrecht, Bill. *Dinner at the New Gene Café.* New York, NY: Thomas Dunne Books, 2001.

Levine, Carol. *Taking Sides: Clashing Views on Controversial Bioethical Issues,* 9th ed. Gilford, CT: McGraw-Hill/ Dushkin, 2001.

Lewontin, R. C., Steven Rose, and Leon J. Kamin. *Not in Our Genes: Biology, Ideology, and Human Nature.* New York, NY: Pantheon Books, 1984.

Mappes, Thomas A., and David Degrazia. *Biomedical Ethics,* 5th ed. New York, NY: McGraw-Hill, 2001.

Monitoring Stem Cell Research; A Report of The President's Council on Bioethics. Washington, DC: www.bioethics.gov, 2004.

Olson, Steve. *Mapping Human History: Genes, Race, and Our Common Origins.* New York, NY: Houghton Mifflin, 2002.

Pence, Gregory. *Cloning After Dolly: Who's Still Afraid?* New York, NY: Rowman & Littlefield Publishers, 2004.

Pence, Gregory. *Who is Afraid of Human Cloning?* New York, NY: Rowman & Littlefield Publishers, 1997.

Preston, Richard. *The Demon in the Freezer.* New York, NY: Random House, 2002.

Preston, Richard. *The Hot Zone.* New York, NY: Anchor Books Doubleday, 1994.

Ridley, Matt. *Genome: The Autobiography of a Species in 23 Chapters.* New York, NY: Harper Collins Publishers, 1999.

Rose, Steven. *Lifelines: Biology Beyond Determinism.* New York, NY: Oxford University Press, 1997.

Rudacille, Deborah. *The Scalpel and the Butterfly: The War between Animal Research and Animal Protection.* New York, NY: Farrar, Straus, and Giroux, 2000.

Silver, Lee M. *Remaking Eden: How Genetic Engineering and Cloning Will Transform the American Family.* New York, NY: Avon Books, 1997.

Stem Cells and the Future of Regenerative Medicine. Washington, DC: National Academy Press, 2002.

Stem Cells: Scientific Progress and Future Research Directions. Bethesda, MD: Report prepared by the National Institutes of Health, 2001

Stock, Gregory. *Redesigning Humans: Choosing Our Genes, Changing Our Future.* New York, NY: Houghton Mifflin, 2002.

Sykes, Bryan. *The Seven Daughters of Eve.* New York, NY: W. W. Norton, 2001.

Thomas, Lewis. *The Lives of a Cell: Notes of a Biology Watcher.* New York, NY: Penguin Books, 1978.

Vatican. "Sacred Congregation For The Doctrine Of The Faith: Declaration On Procured Abortion." Available online at: *http://www.vatican.va/roman_curia/congregations/cfaith/documents/rc_con_cfaith_doc_19741118_declaration-abortion_en.html.*

Veatch, Robert M. *The Basics of Bioethics,* 2nd ed. Pearson Education, 2003.

Watson, James D., and Andrew Berry. *DNA: The Secret of Life.* New York, NY: Alfred A. Knopf, 2004.

Wilmut, Ian, Keith Campbell, and Colin Tudge. *The Second Creation: Dolly and the Age of Biological Control.* Cambridge, MA: Harvard University Press, 2000.

Biotechnology

DeSalle, Rob, and Michael Yudell. *Welcome to the Genome: A Users' Guide to the Genetic Past, Present, and Future.* Hoboken, NJ: John Wiley and Sons, 2005.

Watson, James D., and Andrew Berry. *DNA: The Secret of Life.* New York, NY: Alfred A. Knopf, 2004.

Ethics

Heilbroner, Robert L. *The Worldly Philosophers.* New York, NY: Time Inc, 1962.

Hilts, Philip J. *Protecting America's Health: The FDA, Business, and One Hundred Years of Regulation.* New York, NY: Alfred A. Knopf, 2003.

Veatch, Robert M. *The Basics of Bioethics*, 2nd ed. Pearson Education, 2003.

Animal Cloning

Pence, Gregory. *Cloning After Dolly: Who's Still Afraid?* New York, NY: Rowman & Littlefield Publishers, 2004.

Rudacille, Deborah. *The Scalpel and the Butterfly: The War between Animal Research and Animal Protection.* New York, NY: Farrar, Straus, and Giroux, 2000.

Human Cloning

Pence, Gregory. *Who is Afraid of Human Cloning?* New York, NY: Rowman & Littlefield Publishers, 1997.

Silver, Lee M. *Remaking Eden: How Genetic Engineering and Cloning Will Transform the American Family.* New York, NY: Avon Books, 1997.

Stock, Gregory. *Redesigning Humans: Choosing Our Genes, Changing Our Future.* New York, NY: Houghton Mifflin, 2002.

Stem Cells

Holland, Suzanne, Karen Lebacqz, and Laurie Zoloth. *The Human Embryonic Stem Cell Debate: Science, Ethics, and Public Policy.* Cambridge, MA: MIT Press, 2001.

Monitoring Stem Cell Research; A Report of The President's Council on Bioethics. Washington, DC: *www.bioethics.gov*, 2004.

Stem Cells and the Future of Regenerative Medicine. Washington, DC: National Academy Press, 2002.

Stem Cells: Scientific Progress and Future Research Directions. Bethesda, MD: Report prepared by the National Institutes of Health, 2001.

GMOs

Fumento, Michael. *Bio Evolution: How Biotechnology is Changing Our World.* San Francisco, CA: Encounter Books, 2003.

Lambrecht, Bill. *Dinner at the New Gene Café.* New York, NY: Thomas Dunne Books, 2001.

Biotechnology

http://www.nih.gov/sigs/bioethics/

This Website, created by the National Institutes of Health, contains a broad listing of annotated Web links that provide background information and various positions on issues in bioethics.

http://www.time.com/time/covers/1101030217/scdprofile2.html

Time magazine's Feb. 17, 2003 issue featuring articles on biotechnology's past and future.

http://bancroft.berkeley.edu/ROHO/projects/biosci/symposium/cohen/index.html

"Biotechnology at 25: Perspectives on History, Science, and Society"—a talk by Stanley Cohen at the University of California at Berkeley.

http://www.dnai.org/index.htm

A Website from the Cold Spring Harbor Laboratories Dolan Learning Center that provides excellent learning resources in biotechnology.

Ethics

http://www.bioethics.gov/

Homepage of the President's Council on Bioethics. Includes reports that discuss ethical considerations for many topics in biotechnology. These reports reflect the president's conservative views, but also strive to give honest and balanced treatment to all topics.

http://www.nih.gov/sigs/bioethics/

The National Institutes of Health Website provides a very comprehensive listing of bioethical resources on the Web.

http://www.thehastingscenter.org/default.asp

The Hastings Center is an independent, nonpartisan, and nonprofit bioethics research institute founded in 1969 to explore fundamental and emerging questions in health care, biotechnology, and the environment.

http://www.bio.org/bioethics/links.asp

The Biotechnology Industry Association site has links to many other bioethics sites.

http://www.georgetown.edu/research/nrcbl/nbac/

Reports from President Clinton's National Bioethics Advisory Commission, which last met in 2001.

http://www.conexuspress.com/catalog/golden_rule_workshopweb.htm
A do-it-yourself workshop on the Golden Rule that can be used to help stimulate discussion.

Animal Cloning

http://www.nal.usda.gov/awic/legislat/usdaleg1.htm
Information on laws that address the humane treatment of animals in research.

http://www.animalrights.net/archives/related_topics/organizations/pro_ar/
Comprehensive list of links to animal rights organizations.

http://www.animalrights.net/
AnimalRights.Net is a Website for information and discussion critical of the animal rights movement.

http://bio.p9.org.uk/
A biography of Hans Spemann, who is credited with performing the first cloning experiments on amphibians. Included are excerpts from his laboratory notebooks.

http://www.faseb.org/opar/cloning
A historical timeline of important advances in cloning technology.

http://www.nap.edu/readingroom/books/biomems/rbriggs.html
National Academy of Sciences biography of Robert Briggs who, with Thomas King, developed nuclear transfer technology for use in frogs.

http://intl.pnas.org/cgi/reprint/100/14/8048.pdf
An informative article titled "The First Half-Century of Nuclear Transplant" on the history of this technology, which is used in creating cloned animals.

http://www.accessexcellence.org/WN/SUA09/clone297.html
Access Excellence Website that features articles about the cloning of Dolly the sheep.

http://www.accessexcellence.org/WN/SU/copycat.html
Access Excellence site on cloning of other kinds of animals besides sheep.

Human Cloning

http://www.bioethics.gov/

The homepage for the President's Council on Bioethics.

http://www.bioethics.gov/reports/cloningreport/

The full text of the president's report on human cloning, *Human Cloning and Human Dignity, An Ethical Inquiry.* The President's Council on Bioethics, Washington, D.C., July 2002.

http://www.nih.gov/sigs/bioethics/

A listing of bioethical resources on the Web, which includes some very good resources on the human cloning debate.

http://www.advancedcell.com/

Advanced Cell Technologies is a biotechnology company applying human embryonic stem cell technology in the emerging field of regenerative medicine. This was the first American company to attempt to create human embryos for stem cell research by SCNT.

http://cloninginformation.org/index.html

The Website for the Americans to Ban Cloning (ABC) coalition, a group of concerned American and U.S.-based organizations that promote a comprehensive global ban on human cloning.

http://www.reproductivecloning.net/index.html

The Reproductive Cloning Network is a liberal pro-cloning information site that publishes articles about cloning.

http://www.ncsl.org/programs/health/genetics/rt-shcl.htm

A state-by-state list of cloning laws.

Stem Cells

http://stemcells.nih.gov/index.asp

The official National Institutes of Health resource for stem cell research.

http://www.whitehouse.gov/news/releases/2001/08/20010809-2.html

Remarks by President Bush made in August 2001 about banning stem cell research.

http://www.isscr.org/science/faq.htm

Website for the International Society for Stem Cell Research, an independent, nonprofit organization that shares supportive information on stem cell research.

http://www.news.wisc.edu/packages/stemcells/

A University of Wisconsin-Madison Website with information and recent articles about stem cells.

http://www.stemcellresearchnews.com/

Provides information and includes an extensive list of stem cell–related articles.

http://www.molbio.princeton.edu/courses/mb427/2001/projects/09/SObasics.htm

A good site for basic information on stem cell science.

GMOs

http://www.abcinformation.org/index.php

This site is sponsored by a group of companies that are attempting to win over European trust of genetically modified foods. They try to provide a positive perspective on the issue, but are honest in the information they present.

http://www.gmwatch.org

GMWatch is an organization that distrusts companies producing GMOs and monitors their activities. It presents profiles on the companies and articles that discuss the dangers of GMOs.

http://www.cec.org/maize/

The North American Commission for Environmental Cooperation is composed of representatives from Canada, Mexico, and the United States who work together to assess environmental issues affecting these countries. This site provides a report on the effects of GMO corn on native plants in Mexico.

http://www.biotechknowledge.com/BIOTECH/knowcenter.nsf

A collection of scientific articles that present factual material as well as articles representing a wide range of opinion about GMOs. The site is sponsored by Monsanto, a company that creates and sells GM crops, and is intended to help educate the public about GMOs. Learn how GMOs are created on this site.

http://www.greenpeace.org/international_en/
Homepage for Greenpeace, an organization that strongly opposes GM technology.

http://www.ucsusa.org/
Homepage for the Union of Concerned Scientists, with resources and articles about their concerns regarding GM technology.

http://www.sierraclub.org/
The Sierra Club site includes a way to search for genetic engineering articles presenting their view of this technology.

page:

3: (bottom) © Charles Gupton/ CORBIS

8: Associated Press, AP/Toby Talbot

9: © W. Cody/CORBIS

14: Associated Press, AP/Ken Ruinard

15: © Bettmann/CORBIS

25: © Peter Lamb

33: © Peter Lamb

37: © Peter Lamb

38: © Najlah Feanny/CORBIS

41: © Peter Lamb

44: © Kim Kulish/CORBIS

48: Associated Press, AP/Ralph Raadford

58: © Bettmann/CORBIS

60: © Peter Lamb

72: Associated Press, AP

87: (top) © Dr. David M. Phillips/ Visuals Unlimited

87: (bottom) © Peter Lamb

89: © Peter Lamb

91: Associated Press, AP/Matt Houston

92: © Peter Lamb

102: Associated Press, AP/Mike Derer

106: © AJ/IRRI/CORBIS

110: © Peter Lamb

119: © Science VU/Visuals Unlimited

128: (top) © William Weber/ Visuals Unlimited

JONATHAN MORRIS, PH.D., has been an Associate Professor of Biology at Manchester Community College in Manchester, Connecticut, since 2004. Before moving to Manchester, he was Program Coordinator for the Biotechnology and Environmental Science Programs at Middlesex Community College in Connecticut since 1994. Dr. Morris teaches cell biology, genetics, microbiology, molecular biotechniques, and biochemistry. Dr. Morris received his Ph.D. in Biomedical Sciences from Wright State University in Dayton, Ohio, in 1989. Before accepting the position at Middlesex Community College, Dr. Morris was awarded a three-year post-doctoral fellowship in the Metabolism Training Program at Case Western-Reserve University, and he taught biotechnology at East Carolina University for two years. Dr. Morris has been involved in numerous projects that help educate students in biotechnology. These include the "Shoestring Biotechnology" project, sponsored by the National Science Foundation and National Association of Biology Teachers. He was also an instructor for the PIMMS (Project to Increase the Mastery of Math and Science) and a member of the Biotechnology Professional Development Committee at Wesleyan University. Dr. Morris has worked for C.U.R.E. (Connecticut United for Research Excellence) as the Interim Program Director of the Connecticut BioBus. During the summers, Dr. Morris teaches biotechnology to inner city students in Yale's S.C.H.O.L.A.R.S. Program. Dr. Morris has also participated in summer externships at CuraGen Corp., Monsanto Corp., and the Connecticut Agricultural Experiment Station, where he has gained firsthand knowledge of current trends in biotechnology.